Wells B Fox

What I Remember of the Great Rebellion

Wells B Fox

What I Remember of the Great Rebellion

ISBN/EAN: 9783337207212

Printed in Europe, USA, Canada, Australia, Japan

Cover: Foto ©ninafisch / pixelio.de

More available books at **www.hansebooks.com**

WHAT I REMEMBER

OF THE

GREAT REBELLION

BY

WELLS B. FOX

LATE SURGEON EIGHTH MICHIGAN INFANTRY AND SURGEON-IN-CHIEF
FIELD HOSPITAL, FIRST DIVISION, NINTH ARMY CORPS.

LANSING, MICH.:
DARIUS D. THORP, PRINTER AND BINDER.
1892.

Entered according to Act of Congress, May, 1892, by
WELLS B. FOX, M. D.,
Bancroft, Mich.,
In the Office of the Librarian of Congress, at Washington.

To my comrades of the (six) Michigan regiments who were wounded in the flank movements made by the Army of the Potomac from June 6, 1864, to the close of the rebellion [whose history will herein be found], this volume is affectionately dedicated.

WELLS B. FOX.

WELLS B. FOX,
Surgeon 8th Michigan Infantry.

PREFACE.

IN writing this volume it is with mingled feelings of pleasure and pain that I recall the many incidents that naturally occur in such a scene of the Nation's History as that which I propose to bring to my readers' notice.

I have endeavored to be as plain and simple as possible, recognizing the fact that "simplicity and truth travel hand in hand."

Truth, or the actual facts, should be the first and main object kept constantly in view in writing history.

It cannot reasonably be expected that I can give a detailed account of engagements, the duties I had to perform being of such a character (Surgeon in Chief of Field Hospital) as to divide my attention. But I have endeavored to include in my writings those facts of interest I feel will be recognized by those regiments I have mentioned in connection with the 8th Michigan, whose movements I propose to follow from its conception to their final separation to their homes, many of whom, I regret to say, will languish in pain and suffering for the remainder of their days, but with the consoling thought, which I trust has alleviated many a patriot's suffering, "For my country and my home."

This work will be the more interesting, I trust, from the fact of my being able to publish the names of the wounded and the nature of their injuries in the various engagements as they occurred, the details of which I have in my office today as recorded during the war by my assistant, which I revere as a sacred relic of the war between the North and South, to determine that the flag of this country should float over the "free," without respect to color or race.

WELLS B. FOX.

E. J. BONINE,
Surgeon 2d Michigan Infantry.

When deadly foemen meet in strife,
Both equally brave and daring,
One or the other falls and leaves
A sad history behind him.
But 'tis worse when brother holds
A knife 'gainst brother's throat
And challenges him to fight him.
One holds the flag, the emblem of our nation,
Whose stars are all in glory set,
The other would destroy them.

CONTENTS.

Chapter I.

Names of companies and where formed — Grand Rapids — Fort Wayne — Names of field and staff officers — Leaving Detroit — Washington — Meridian Hill — Annapolis — Orders for Hilton Head — Beaufort — Ladies Island — Brickyard Point — Shell Road — Gray's Hill Plantation — The flag — Steamer Honduras — Wilmington Island — On board the Alabama — Metland — Stone River — Secessionville — Hilton Head — Beaufort — On board the Vanderbilt — Fortress Monroe — Newport News — Aqua Creek — Fredericksburg — Culpepper — Through Alexandria — Washington — Frederick City and Middleton — Lieut. Belcher — Sharpsburg — Harper's Ferry — Fredericksburg — Waterford — Falmouth — Newport News — Louisville, Kentucky — Lebanon — Vicksburg — Middledale — Flowerdale Church — Jackson — A lousy regiment — Yazoo — Cairo — Cincinnati — Morristown, twenty thousand miles — Blue Springs — Sam Jones — Burnside — Greenville — Andrew Johnson — A. Johnson, tailor — The raider — Horses eat oats — Soldiers eat soup — Major W. E. Lewis — Knoxville — Louden — Bricks that walk — From Louden to Campbell Station — Twelve thousand men hold thirty-six thousand — The graves at Campbell Station — Cumberland Gap — Three thousand prisoners.

Chapter II.

Capt. Roemer — National Encampment, Detroit — Lieut. Benjamin — Fort Sanders — The attack — Keep cool, Doctor — An old enemy — Face to face — Repulse of Longstreet — Arrival of Sherman — Blaine's X Roads — Re-enlist and furlough — Address to the 79th New York Highlanders — Homeward bound — Baker and the mule hides — Old John Brown — Cumberland Gap — The sutler — Informed against — Tell the sutler to get out — Barbersville — Rawhide moccasins for twelve-dollar boots — Cheese and chickens — Delos Warner — A good time — Big Log mountain — Death of the teamster — Crab Orchard — 10th Mich. Cavalry — Col. Trowbridge — Martin Decker — At Fenton — In barracks at Flint.

Chapter III.

Danford Parker — Col. Fenton — Drummer boy's mother — To the front again — Louisville — Annapolis — Chesapeake Bay — Fresh arrivals — Grant made lieutenant general — Measles — George Griswold — Dwight Skinner — The funeral service — Capt. R. M. Doyle — Col. Ely — Reviewed by Lincoln — Fairfax — Centreville — Warrington Station — Rappahannock Station — Germania Ford — The horse and its rider fell into the water — Wilderness Run — Col. F. Graves — Battle of Wilderness — Names of wounded — Lost half the regiment — Capt. Hutchinson — Chancellorsville — The wounded to Fredericksburg — Water, water — Dying from thirst — Exit 24th — Capt. James Donahue.

Chapter IV.

Lieut. Hovey — The Wounded of the 8th Mich. at Spottsylvania — Come, first brigade — Morrison wounded — Laing — Baird — Gaird — Those Scotchmen — I will fight it out, etc. — The wounded taken to Fredericksburg — Records retained — Meade versus Sheridan — List of wounded at battle of Spottsylvania — Face to face again — Forward — Insubordination — Wounded at Cold Harbor.

Chapter V.

The James — Sleep a luxury — To the front again — Hot work — Wounded at Petersburg — Lieut. Campbell — Bull-dog grip — The mine — Richard Vickery.

Chapter VI.

Weldon Railroad — The surprise — To the rescue — The wounded at Weldon Railroad — Major Belcher — The wounded at Poplar Grove Church — Presidential election — All men equal before the law — Proclamation of emancipation — A billion dollars —

A living lie — Shelling day and night — The wounded on vidette and picket duty — Wounded during fall of Petersburg — Surgeon Bonine — Dr. Aaron Vanderveene — Dr. Fitch — Dr. Sherlock — Deep Bottoms — Weldon Railroad — Hatchers Run — A cyclone — The country paralyzed — Stevens, Campbell and Hunter — Sent to Hampton Roads — The interview — Shall they hold the right of franchise — Root, hog, or die.

Chapter VII.

Britain's premier — Disraeli — Miners and farmers — Gen. Hartranft — Charge — Pennsylvanians, do your duty — A bloody scene — Shenandoah — Sheridan — Slavery declared piracy — An eternal lie — Had a friend in the hospital — Gen. Wilcox — Campus Martius — 79th New York Highlanders — Morrison — Laing — Moore — Col. Ely — Sherman on to the sea — Gen. Butler — Wilmington — Heavy firing at the front — Crossing the Weldon Railroad — Death or victory — Closer and closer — Close up — Mad Phil — A raging lion — The coffee — Dr. G. McDonald — A contemptible brute — An anxious night — Twenty long hours — Swore and ripped and tore — Relief of Gen. Warren — Five Forks — A grand success — Cavalry in a new phase.

Chapter VIII.

Jeff Davis — The devil and his minions — Chief Justice Taney — An infamous decision — A peg in his wheel — Forks of the Deatonsfield road — Confederate losses at Sailors Creek — The decisive point — Forty thousand Enfield rifles — Heavy roads — Sufferings of wounded — Succoring the rebs — What will "you uns" do with "we uns" — One thousand wounded in hospital — Assassination of Lincoln — Vengeance on the rebs — Feelings mollified — Strike tents — On a visit — Glad the war is over — Murdered — Back to Washington — Burial of the president — Georgetown — Tennallytown — Growing restless — Tied up by the thumbs — Drunk — Tie him up — Surgeon-in-chief — Two barrels of beer.

Chapter IX.

The pigs and cows — Capt. Hovey — Leakage in stores — Self-preservation — Goodies — Mustered out.

Chapter X.

The flag — "My country, 'tis of thee" — Four millions of human beings — Last expiring breath — The oppressed of all nations — Homeward bound — Breakfast — Cleveland — Detroit — The chaplain, George Taylor — A legacy.

Chapter XI.

Names of sick.

Chapter XII.

Names of 8th Mich. Infantry living.

Chapter XIII.

Commissioned officers.

Appendix.

The reunion at Detroit — Comrade Hutchinson's poem — The drummer boy of the Rappahannock.

COL. W. M. FENTON,
8th Michigan Infantry.

CHAPTER I.

The 8th Michigan Infantry was formed and companies assigned August 12, 1861, and were recruited, as near as I can ascertain the facts, as follows:

Co.	Name of Company.	Where Recruited.
A	Fenton Light Guards	Flint.
B	St. Johns Volunteers	St. Johns.
C	Gratiot Rangers	Alma.
D	Grand River Guards	Grand Rapids.
E	Elder Zouaves	Lansing.
F		Hastings.
G	Excelsior Guards	Flint.
H	Greenville Guards	Greenville.
I		Owosso.
K		Jackson.

The regiment was, on August 21, 1861, ordered to rendezvous at Grand Rapids, where they reported to Colonel W. M. Fenton of Flint, who had been formerly Major of the 7th Michigan Infantry.

From Grand Rapids we were ordered to Fort Wayne, arriving there September 16, where the regiment completed its organization and was mustered into the United States Army on the same day.

The following are the names of the field and staff officers of the 8th Michigan Infantry.

Colonel, William M. Fenton of Fenton.
Lieutenant Colonel, Frank Graves of Niles.
Major, Amasa B. Watson of Muskegon.
Surgeon, Hulburt B. Shank of Lansing.
Assistant Surgeon, Samuel R. Wooster of Grand Rapids.
Adjutant, David B. Harbaugh of Detroit.
Quartermaster, Asa Gregory of Flint.
Chaplain, William Mahon of Detroit.

COMPANY A.

Captain, Samuel C. Guild of Flint.
First Lieutenant, George Newell of Flint.
Second Lieutenant, George H. Turner of Flint.

COMPANY B.

Captain, Gilbert E. Pratt of Detroit.
First Lieutenant, William E. Lewis of St. Johns.
Second Lieutenant, James S. Donahue of Flint.

COMPANY C.

Captain, Ralph Ely of Alma.
First Lieutenant, George S. Gordon of Alma.
Second Lieutenant, Charles B. Holliday of Alma.

COMPANY D.

Captain, Benjamin B. Church of Grand Rapids.
First Lieutenant, John C. Buchanan of Grand Rapids.
Second Lieutenant, Benjamin F. Porter of Grand Rapids.

HULBERT B. SHANK,
Surgeon 8th Michigan Infantry.

COMPANY E.

Captain, Mathew Elder of Lansing.
First Lieutenant, Abraham Cottrell of Lansing.
Second Lieutenant, Nelson Chapman, Lansing.

COMPANY F.

Captain, Nelson H. Walbridge of Richland.
First Lieutenant, Traverse Phillips of Hastings.
Second Lieutenant, Jacob Maus of Hastings.

COMPANY G.

Captain, Ephraim N. Lyon of Flint.
First Lieutenant, Horatio Belcher of Flint.
Second Lieutenant, N. Miner Pratt of Flint.

COMPANY H.

Captain, Alfred B. Turner of Grand Rapids.
First Lieutenant, Richard N. Doyle of Georgetown.
Second Lieutenant, William A. Brown of Ann Arbor.

COMPANY I.

Captain, Jay L. Quackenbush of Owosso.
First Lieutenant, Albert Bainbridge of Byron.
Second Lieutenant, James C. Merrell of Corunna.

COMPANY K.

Captain, George Proudfit of Jackson.
First Lieutenant, Reuben S. Cheney of Moscow.
Second Lieutenant, William P. Miner of Moscow.

The 8th Michigan Infantry has been "dubbed" the "Wandering Regiment" of Michigan, the appropriateness of which will be manifest to my readers as they notice the various long-distance marches and counter-marches they made and the number of battles in which they were engaged, having been as early as November, 1862, in engagements in South Carolina, Georgia, Virginia and Maryland, and in 1863 in Mississippi and Tennessee.

The regiment moved from Detroit on September 27, 1861, in command of Colonel Fenton, with a roll call of a little over nine hundred men (915). Arriving at Washington on September 30 they went into camp on Meridian Hill.

On October 9, the regiment left for Annapolis, Maryland, arriving there on the morning of the 10th, where it was assigned to duty as a part of the first brigade under General Isaac Stevens, at that time under orders for Hilton Head.

Joining the other regiments they went into camp on the 10th of the same month, where they were kept busy throwing up earthworks and doing picket duty until December 6, 1861, when they took up their line of march with the brigade, boarding steamers at Hilton Head, and were conveyed to Beaufort the next day where they bivouacked until the 9th of December, when they pitched their tents and commenced the monotony of drill and picket duty.

Lieutenant Porter occupied Ladies Island, and Captain Elder was stationed at Brickyard Point. Lieutenant Porter, ever anxious for a scrimmage, surprised and took some few prisoners on the 18th of December, when the regiment shifted its quarters to about six miles from Beaufort, on the Shell Road.

On the 21st they moved with the 79th New York, formed the advance posts in command of Colonel Fenton, and on the 22d moved to Gray's Hill Plantation, where they remained until the 31st of December, 1861.

From January 1, 1862, until March, there is nothing particular outside of a few minor "brushes" with the enemy to record. But the time was occupied in bringing both men and officers to a higher point of proficiency.

During this period it is very gratifying to note the people of Genesee county presented to the regiment a beautiful flag, which was presented by General Isaac I. Stevens in behalf of the citizens of that county.

On the 16th of April, 1862, seven companies of

four hundred men each were taken on board the steamer "Honduras," bound for Wilmington Island, where they had a short but sharp conflict with the enemy, thoroughly routing them, insomuch that they left their dead upon the field. During the remainder of April and May the regiment remained on Port Royal Island.

On June 1, early in the morning, they embarked on board the gunboat "Alabama," below Beaufort, and lay at Hilton Head and steamed off Stone river. On the 3d they were transferred to the "Metland," thence up Stone river, and landed and bivouacked.

On the 7th of June they were attached to the first brigade, together with the 7th Connecticut and 28th Massachusetts, under the command of Colonel Fenton, while the regiment, commanded by Colonel F. Graves, showed what fighting material they were composed of in the assault on the enemy's works at Secessionville.

On July 5 the regiment left James Island for Hilton Head, and on the 10th left for Beaufort, and on the 13th embarked on the steamer "Vanderbilt" for Fortress Monroe, and, landing at Newport News, went into camp on the 17th of July.

On August 4 we left Newport News for Aqua

Creek, thence to Fredericksburg, Culpepper, Raccoon Ford, Kelley's Ford, Sulphur Springs, Warren Station, Manassas Station and Centreville.

Immediately following these battles the regiment, in command of Major Ralph Ely, moved on the Maryland campaign, marching via Alexandria, Washington, Frederick City and Middleton, Maryland, and became heavily engaged at South Mountain on the 14th of September, where Lieutenant Belcher so signally maintained the character (so well earned) of the 8th Michigan Infantry that had ever been theirs.

Lieutenant Belcher's conduct was so gallant that he was especially mentioned in General I. D. Cox's report, as follows:

"I cannot close this report without speaking of the meritorious conduct of First Lieutenant H. Belcher of the 8th Michigan Infantry, a regiment belonging to another division.

"His regiment having suffered severely on the right, and being partly thrown into confusion, he rallied about one hundred men and led them up to the front. Being separated from the brigade to which he belonged, he reported to me for duty, and asked for a position where he could be of use until his proper place could be ascertained.

"He was assigned a post on the left, and subsequently in support of the advance section of Simmon's battery, in both of which places he and his men performed their duty admirably, and after the repulse of the enemy in the evening, he carried his command to their proper brigade."

On the 19th of September the regiment commenced its march back into Virginia again by way of Sharpsburg and Harper's Ferry.

On the 24th Colonel Fenton returned to the regiment and assumed command of the first brigade, while Major Ely was in command of the 8th Michigan.

The regiment left Waterford, Va., on the 2d of November, 1862, and arrived at Falmouth on the 18th, where it lay until the 12th of December, doing provost duty for its division. It crossed with the army to Fredericksburg, but sustained no loss in the battle at that place. It remained near Falmouth until the 13th of February, 1863, when it moved to Newport News, encamping there until the 19th of March. Again embarking, it proceeded, via Baltimore, to Louisville, Ky., and thence to Lebanon, Ky. Remaining there until June, it moved, in command of Colonel Frank Graves, to Vicksburg with the Ninth Army Corps, going into camp at Middledale, near Vicksburg, on the 17th. It was stationed at Middledale and Flowerdale Church where I reported for duty and assumed the responsibilities of a surgeon in chief.

From this point in the history of the 8th Michigan regiment I propose to give a more detailed account of what occurred, being present myself, and right here I desire to publicly thank my numerous friends and correspondents who have so willingly aided me in compiling this valuable little work.

Just prior to the attack on Jackson, Miss., I caught up with the main body of the command. The regiment had had no surgeon of full rank for a considerable time, and I found them the most dirty, lousy, and dilapidated lot of men it had ever been my fortune to meet in the service.

Anticipating somewhat their condition, I had provided myself with comforts obtained from the Christian Commission, so that I was able on my first introduction to render them substantial aid in time of need, which I believe was duly appreciated.

When I look back and think of their condition, and see some of them living here today, the contrast is indeed striking. The friendship we formed the first twenty-four hours I was with them has grown stronger and stronger with the lapse of time. The duties we were called upon to perform were thoroughly accomplished in driving Johnston from the Mississippi and in the destruction of many miles of the Mobile & Alabama railroad, when we returned to the Yazoo and took steamer for Cairo, Ill., whence, by rail, we were soon landed in Cincinnati, Ohio, and entered on the campaign of East Tennessee, reaching Morristown, on the line of the Virginia & East Tennessee railroad, early in October—having made a circuit of over twenty thousand miles by marching and counter-marching. No corps in the service to this date had been required to make the sacrifices that the 8th, 2d, 17th, 20th and 27th Michigan regiments, in connection with regiments from other states, had cheerfully given for their country.

A few days later, in connection with the Twenty-third Army Corps, we were marched eastward to help the Army of the Ohio out of a snap at Blue Springs, October 10, 1863. It was laughable to witness the consternation of the new troops in this action (they being for the first time under fire), as they ran to and fro trying to hold Sam Jones in check. In the midst of the fight General Burnside rode into our lines, yelling, "Michigan men, go and drive

Jones out of those woods!" which was quickly done, and to his satisfaction.

The night of this day was passed unmolested by the rebels, but on the following day we pursued them as far as Greenville, the home of ex-President Andrew Johnson, in whose dooryard the 8th Michigan proceeded to establish their headquarters.

At that date Greenville had a population not exceeding three thousand inhabitants, and on the principal street was a story and a half brick house and a small building, on the front door of which was the sign, "A. JOHNSON, TAILOR."

This same dooryard proved to be the place where the 10th Michigan Cavalry, a year later, brought John Morgan, the illustrious raider, to his final halt.

That little brick house and that little office, which are remembered so well by hundreds of Michigan troops, was the home of ex-President Andrew Johnson of impeachment fame.

We marched a few miles eastward during the cool of the evening and went into camp, but our commissary stores and quartermaster did not come up until midnight. A few of the boys had a little coffee and a small quantity of hard-tack, which they cheerfully divided with each other—officers and men alike. We were faint and thoroughly exhausted from the terrible experience through which we had passed, and I well remember our major quoting BONAPARTE as having said, "Horses must have oats," and BLUCHER, that "Soldiers must have soup."

I had attained to nearly forty years of age, but my dear and intimate friend, Major W. E. Lewis, who fell at the battle of Cold Harbor, was sick and worn and suffered much from the heavy dews that fall at that season of the year in East Tennessee. Previous to my army experience I had become inured to exposure and could endure more than most men, but I felt for him, under such trying circumstances. Major Lewis rose to his rank by virtue of no friend or favor, but by pure and indomitable bravery on the field of battle. When he entered the service he held the position of chief accountant in one of the leading mercantile houses in St. Johns, Michigan (Fish & Sons). I remember when his application for leave of absence was sent in for approval that he might purchase a new flag for the regiment and pay a short visit to his young wife. Major Lewis was one of the most cultured, moral, and noble young men of that grand galaxy of youthful heroes which Michigan sent to the war in 1861.

MAJOR W. ELY LEWIS,
Killed at Cold Harbor, Va., June 3, 1864.

How could we fail? It was not possible, the reason being apparent: the first five hundred thousand men who volunteered to serve their country and save its flag were impelled by the richest elements of patriotism. Other patriots have and will make as great sacrifices for home and country as did my youthful friend, but no purer, better blood was ever shed than that poured out by W. E. Lewis on the morning of the 3d of June, 1864, at Cold Harbor.

> Memorial days shall come and go,
> And flowers shall bloom each year,
> But nature bringeth not a hue
> I would not place upon thy bier.

Early the following morning General Burnside ordered the Army of the Ohio to retreat rapidly to Knoxville, and thence to Louden, on the Tennessee River, a point it was designed we should hold (did not the enemy disturb us) until the following spring, when active military operations could, with prudence, be attempted.

The two divisions of the Ninth Army Corps set about building for themselves winter quarters, and many episodes occurred of a truly laughable character. I call to mind one, where a mill had been burned, in the construction of which several thousand bricks had been used, which our division quartermaster, George Baker, sought to divide equally among the regiments of the old division. Poor Baker was a good, clever fellow, but he was not able, however well he attempted to do his duty, to divide those bricks. The 8th and 2d Michigan could out-Herod Herod, out-wit and out-steal all such men as poor Baker. The 2d *at first* got more brick than the 8th. The 79th got more than the 8th and the 2d put together; but when the shades of night settled o'er the camp, if one had eyes sharp enough, they would have seen bricks with legs, and hands, too; for they were moving across that camp ground as fast as any one man could walk, all the men lying flat and passing brick by brick until the *chimneys* of the 79th New York Highlanders and the 2d Michigan Infantry had *shifted quarters*.

Captain Armor of the 79th New York Highlanders was a noble representative of Scotia's sons, and when he met the 8th on the "Vanderbilt" he thought they were a green lot of "Wolverines," and so they were. And yet we taught him, officer of the day as he was, although we did not understand the pocketpicking tactics of Tammany and Brooklyn (with which he may have been familiar), that we could steal him, his regiment, "Papa" Fitch, and all the *corn meal* they had.

The 79th New York Highlanders and the 8th Michigan Infantry loved each other better than any other regiments of Burnside's Ninth Army Corps. The 79th saved us at James Island, and we saved them at Spottsylvania. They saved us again at Nye River, and we did not forget them at that terrible charge at Fort Mahon. Those Scotchmen—God bless them— Morrison, Moore, Armor, Todd and all the others of that noble band of patriots will ever live in the memories of the 8th Michigan Infantry.

While we were so pleasantly situated, enjoying the rest we so much needed, news of the defeat of General Rosecranz at Chickamauga reached us, putting the Army of the Ohio on the *qui vive.*

At this time we had not rations for more than fifteen days, no railroad connections, or other adequate transportation for supplies. Perhaps at no other period in the history of the war was an army so situated as we were at Knoxville in 1863.

We fell back from Louden to Campbell Station, a little hamlet about twenty miles from

Knoxville, established our lines and held, with twelve thousand men, Longstreet's corps of thirty-six thousand until evening. There are graves at Campbell Station filled with men from the 2d, 8th, 17th and 20th Michigan Infantry, 100th Pennsylvania and 79th New York Highlanders; and although they are not marked with marble or bronze, yet their memories are perpetuated in the annals of the heroes of America, who shed their life's blood to win back and save to the Union such portions of this fair country as East Tennessee, which today is giving to the republic more wealth, by her mines of coal and iron, than the Keystone State will ever be able to furnish.

East Tennessee had been regarded by the north as Britons regarded Switzerland. So, indeed, it was prior to the war, but after the destruction of slavery, and that "sum of all villianies" was driven out, a full tide of a new and better light was let in, viz: ALL MEN ARE EQUAL BEFORE THE LAW.

With that heaven-born inspiration those hills and rocks poured forth their wealth.

Cumberland Gap, a rugged pathway where we captured over three thousand rebel troops when we broke their Alpine fastnesses, from a few log cabins has grown to be a city equal to what Atlanta was prior to the first gun fired at Sumter.

CHAPTER II.

Captain Roemer was one of America's adopted sons of whom our corps was deservedly proud. Captain Roemer was looked upon as General Burnside's right-hand man on especial occasions. Roemer, Benjamin and Edwards were the artillerists of the Ninth Army Corps.

Wilcox, Potter and Farrero were in command of a body of men of whom I shall give in this volume a correct record of the casualties which occurred from the time they crossed the Rapidan until Lee's final surrender at Appomattox, so far as relates to the Field Hospital, first division, Ninth Army Corps.

Prince Frederick Charles, when Sheridan visited him, said of Roemer, "That man's great-grandfather was the best artilleryman my nation has ever produced." Certainly, Wilhelm Roemer of our army seemed to us to be the embodiment of all that was required in that arm of the service.

His batteries at the siege of Knoxville were placed on the south side of the Holstein, and when Longstreet ordered McLaws to make his furious charge on Fort Sanders, the wily Dutchman had his eye well "peeled," and dropped into that ditch such a whirlwind of iron that it saved East Tennessee to the Union.

Captain Roemer still lives in New York, and when he visted the 8th Michigan at the national encampment at Detroit, in August, 1891, and we saw him walk up Woodward avenue, his head grown gray with age, we could not but recall the days of his prime, when he, with us, was on the battlefield ready to do and to dare.

Roemer loved the flag. It was his ideal, no matter how rough the roads or perilous the duty; he seemed to know nothing but to obey orders. And I have often thought, as I have attentively studied the history of the Ninth Army Corps, that to the conduct of Captain Roemer's battery is due a large amount of credit for the victories which we achieved in the various battles fought during that campaign.

Lieutenant Benjamin's battery was placed in the fort at Knoxville after the battle of Campbell Station, having lost the day previous quite a number of his caissons Lieutenant Benjamin was quite a young man, having anything but a strong constitution, but was possessed of courage to almost any degree. He requested a detail of forty men (which he obtained) from the old 79th to handle his batteries, purchased a box of cigars, and swore in the language of Andrew Jackson that Fort Sanders should never be taken.

The fort was very poorly provisioned, and the ammunition for the guns, if possible, more so, having about a hundred and twenty shells and two boxes of matches (in my overcoat pocket). Those shells he filled, and cutting the fuse just long enough, dropped them into the ditch, where they immediately exploded, thus effectually preventing McLaws from gaining his parapet.

The slaughter that brave boy caused among those who sought to drive him from Fort Sanders on that damp, cold November morning has never been correctly described by any of the various writers of that event. I shall never forget him as he stood there lighting the fuse and dropping the shells into the ditch, and said, full of the inspiration of fight: "Step a little back, Doctor, keep cool, don't wet, and well-light the matches, and no rebel shall get inside this fort."

Could my readers today get a glimpse at those devil-daring, determined and brave men composing McLaw's division of Georgians, and of the less than seventy-five in the fort, they might get some idea of the work we had in hand.

Benjamin held his fort, Knoxville was saved, and, except a little raiding by *guerrillas*, that great stretch of country of which we have spoken has ever since been free, loyal, and true to the Union.

Perhaps no epoch in the history of Mr. Lincoln's administration gave greater satisfaction to the American people than did this success, which we believe to be the turning point in the great rebellion.

The president was weighed down with anxiety for fear we should be annihilated. But under the guidance of such men as Burnside, with the assistance of Roemer, Benjamin, Edwards, Farrero, and such fighting material as the 2d, 8th, 17th, 20th and 27th Michigan, the 36th Massachusetts, the 79th New York and the 100th Pennsylvanians, and 50th and 51st from the same state, we felt quite capable of at least holding our own, when we remembered that we were men of whom it could be truly said—what NAPOLEON BONAPARTE said of the English—"They never know when they are whipped."

No, sir, the two old divisions of the Ninth Army Corps never knew defeat. They had in their front an old and not to be despised foe, whom they well understood from past experience. Longstreet's men and the Ninth Army Corps had been face to face before, and it so happened at Knoxville, as on many another hard-fought battlefield—we made it a drawn fight.

The corps of General Longstreet, composed of Georgians, Mississippians and Louisianians, was a brave body of men, and if any of our boys fell, by accident of war, into their hands, as far as I had opportunity of observing and hearing, they were always treated kindly. Certainly, I am not cognizant of any man of the Ninth Army Corps receiving any unusually hard fare at their hands, and, although I am aware much has been said and written in regard to the il'-treatment of prisoners of war, I feel grateful that I can testify, to the humanity of our opponents with but one exception, that of the regiments from South Carolina.

The repulse of Longstreet at Fort Sanders and the arrival of Sherman from Chattanooga put an entirely different complexion upon the campaign of East Tennessee.

Early in December, 1863, our division took

up its line of march eastward, along the line of the East Tennessee & Virginia railroad. We had frequent skirmishes with Longstreet's forces, but no general engagement. We encamped at Blaine's X Roads January 1, 1864, where a general order was received from the War Department, to the effect that: "The men of those regiments whose terms expire within a year may re-enlist and proceed to their homes on a furlough of thirty days." Nearly all of the 8th Michigan immediately re-enlisted, and by the morning of the 8th of January, 1864, were ready to start over the Cumberland mountains.

The 8th day of January, 1864, was and still is a memorable day for the 8th Michigan and our old friends of the 79th New York Highlanders. A committee was appointed to draft resolutions expressing our attachment to our old friends, which we presented, reading as follows:

8TH MICHIGAN VETERAN VOLUNTEERS,
BLAINE'S X ROADS, TENN., *January 8, 1864.*

"*Colonel Morrison, Officers and Soldiers:*

"We part with you this cold, bleak January morning with feelings of sadness, such as friends can only feel when parting with friends whom their hearts have learned to love and cherish.

"Every man of your number is made dearer

to us, when we call to mind the many long and blood-stained campaigns through which we have passed, side by side.

"In all our privations, in all our battles, and in all our victories, we have ever been shoulder to shoulder and shared them alike.

"Officers and soldiers of the 79th, we feel proud that it has been our lot to be so closely associated with men so generous, so noble and brave.

"The nation delights to own you as her heroes, Scotia as her children; and the old Empire state, too, feels proud of her Highlanders, and prouder still will she be when historians write your true record.

"It is, therefore, with feelings of deepest regret that we part with you, and we, as a regiment have

"Resolved, That we hereby tender to Colonel David Morrison our heartfelt thanks for the kind manner in which he has seen fit to notice us in special order No. 4, for conduct while under his command. His name shall ever live in our memories.

"Resolved, That we part with the 79th New York Highlanders as brother parteth with brother."

(Signed by the Committee.)

The regiments were drawn up in line, and upon the reading of the above address the order was given and we immediately turned our faces homeward.

It was a cold, stormy morning, and very few

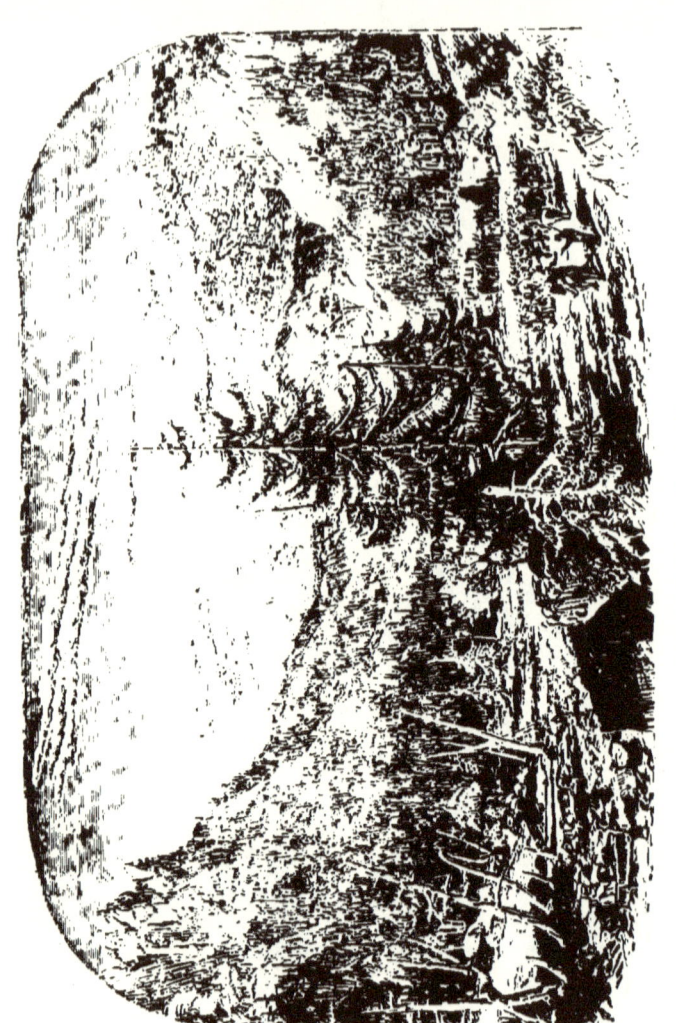
CUMBERLAND GAP.

of the men had shoes suitable for the trying march before us.

Quartermaster Baker gathered all the hides of mules and other animals he could find and had shoes or moccasins made, but as they were untanned and the ground frozen almost as hard as rock, they were soon badly worn and cut to pieces by the stones, and it was no unusual thing to be able to track our boys by the bloody marks of their feet along the road. But we were coming home to Michigan, to visit our friends and families, and no ordinary obstacle could dampen our ardor or impede our progress. Though our sufferings were great and rations poor, we scaled those rocky peaks singing "Old John Brown," "The Star Spangled Banner," etc., the stimulus of which helped us wonderfully on our way.

We reached Cumberland Gap about the 12th of January, 1864, where we met a sutler well supplied with sundries, from officers' clothing down to canned fruit. We were a pack of hungry *wolves*, tired and exhausted, and this was a golden opportunity to supply some of our needs. So a requisition was quickly made upon him, which he declined to grant, but those boots, that cheese, and that brandy, we were bound to have.

I had a hospital fund to the credit of the 8th Michigan Infantry of several hundred dollars, and offered him an order upon Lieutenant Wells, our commissary, for pay for all we took, which he declined to receive. We therefore said to him: "*When we strike you again we will make it all right,*" and helped ourselves.

After we reached Annapolis, the following spring, I found complaint had been made of our conduct at Cumberland Gap to General Burnside, who sent for me and inquired into the matter. I told him what our condition was at the time, assured him that the order I tendered the sutler was correct, and that I had sufficient funds in the hands of the commissary to pay him for all we had taken. The General replied, "If the commissary fund is not good, what the devil is? Go back, Surgeon, to your hospital, and attend to your duties."

Recalling me, he inquired what I had done with my hospital fund. I replied, with hat in hand, "General, you know what I had to do with it. I had nothing to do with it. After it remained in the hands of the commissary for a certain period it had to be turned over, by order of the War Department, to the general hospital fund." Turning his head to his chief of staff

(Colonel Louis Richmond), he said, "When that sutler calls again, say to him that Fox of the 8th Infantry did just right, and a sutler ought to know when a surgeon of his standing in my corps gives an order upon a commissary that it is good only for so many days after it is issued. I am not going to scold Fox for taking good care of his men; he was too faithful in East Tennessee. *Tell the sutler to get out."*

Colonel Ralph Ely fully sustained my action the following evening and corroborated my statement. The sutler probably regarded the bill settled, and I heard no more of that little matter.

Our route was through Cumberland Gap to Barbersville, crossing the Wild Cat Mountains. And perhaps no section of this country is so well watered as East Tennessee and Southern Kentucky. Clear spring water gushing out of the mountain sides almost every mile as you travel.

After leaving Cumberland Gap that memorable 12th of January, made so by our boys exchanging rawhide moccasins for officers boots worth ten dollars per pair, with over four hundred cans of peaches and eight or ten boxes of good Hamburgh cheese, and seizing all the poultry within our reach, it needs no questioning that by the aid of Delos Warner, who possessed a wonderful faculty of finding out and bringing in all the "goodies" for miles around, that we spent one refreshing night in eating, drinking, and sleeping.

Delos Warner, of Company B, seemed to possess a special faculty of bringing new life to us on occasions of deepest gloom. He could feed us better than any quartermaster, he could sing songs and hymns to suit any occasion, and I think the regiment is indebted to him for many an hour which was to us like an oasis in the desert.

In continuing our journey we found that what was a blessing in summer was anything but that in winter, for the clear sparkling liquid had turned to a glare of treacherous, slippery ice. This being the case, my readers will recognize without any great army experience the difficulties attending our trains in moving from place to place at that season of the year. The method we adopted was to attach a rope to the hind end of the wagons, a company or two of the men holding back on the rope, and thus lower them down the mountain side.

Near Big Log Mountain, about the 15th of

January, one of our teamsters in charge of the supply-wagon ignored the help of the men and started to drive down the mountain alone. The road was only about twelve feet wide, winding along the side of the mountain, forming a sort of embankment. He started fairly well, but had not traveled far ere we heard a shout, and saw a lot of slipping and sliding mules and a wagon skidding over the mountain side. The next view was the mules, teamster and wagon lying in the stillness of death at the base of that rugged and dangerous mountain. 'Twas truly sad to part with a comrade without an attempt even to give him sepulture, but necessity knows no law, so we went on our way, having received another of those sad lessons of foolhardiness, that are so common in times of danger.

This wild and mountainous region, as we have before noticed, very much resembles the Swiss Alps, and oh! how glad the boys all were when we began to descend into the bluegrass regions of Kentucky.

We reached Crab Orchard, in Southern Kentucky, the 20th day of January, 1864, after accomplishing one of the many difficult and arduous marches to which we were becoming accustomed, the sufferings from which, I think, will not soon be forgotten by any who took part in it.

The 10th Michigan Cavalry were protecting Central Kentucky at this time, and were stationed at Camp Nelson. Their scouts had learned of our condition, and their commanding officer, Colonel Luther Trowbridge, sent to Crab Orchard two hundred horses to help our poor, suffering boys on their homeward march. The help was timely, and many a silent blessing was offered for the instigator of this generous act, bringing to our minds the truth of the old adage:

"A friend in need
Is a friend indeed."

Among the many who brought the horses to Crab Orchard, that I remember, was one Jefferson Kent of Company H, 10th Michigan Cavalry, who has since then been an invalid for twenty-five years, resulting from injuries received during the various engagements which occurred in East Tennessee.

It is morally impossible, after thirty years, for me to preserve a perfect picture of all of the brave boys who scaled the rugged peaks of Little and Big Log Mountains, forded the Clynch and forced their way onward to the Big Broad of East Tennessee. But it gratifies me to be able to present the photograph of one

JEFFERSON KENT,
10th Michigan Cavalry.

who still lives and is among the well-known and respected citizens of Shiawassee county.

We reached Cincinnati, Ohio, January 25, where the regiment was mustered and paid off.

Freshly clothed, we took cars for Detroit, where we were furloughed to our homes.

One man, a citizen of Antrim, of Company D, whose name was Martin Decker, suffered terribly from chronic diarrhea and the general debility that necessarily follows from a lengthened attack of this disease, more especially in the months of June and July, in Mississippi, and although he knew it was my wish that he should go to the rear hospital, he, like many others, desired to do his duty as a soldier as long as nature would permit.

I secured Decker early in November, at Blue Springs, leave of absence for thirty days. Knowing his leave would expire before the regiment reached home, I wrote to him from East Tennessee, telling him to rest contented and not worry about his furlough having expired, for I should soon be home and would see that it was extended, and no trouble should come of his having remained where he was.

There were at this time scattered over this country a *noble body of sharks*, who made their living by taking advantage of such opportunities as this I mention to inform the Provost Marshal of such men as Decker, causing their arrest, and they would walk off with thirty dollars as a reward for their miserable treachery. Decker shared in the affliction of hundreds of our men, who, through disease, were unable to report before the expiration of their furloughs. The Decker family is remembered today by many of the older citizens of the community in which they reside, and of this incident which I record. George and William Decker, his two brothers, laid their lives on the altar for their country's sake, and what more can a man do for his home, friends, or country.

I remember, on my way to Flint to rejoin the regiment at the expiration of leave of absence, meeting Decker at a hotel in Fenton. As he sat in that hotel, under arrest (more fit to be in bed than on duty), with the vulture eye of that "limb of the law" upon him, Decker said to me:

"How about this, Surgeon?"

"About what?" said I.

"Why, this man has arrested me as a deserter, and I came here for the purpose of meeting you today, and, Surgeon, if you think I am able to rejoin my company I am ready to do so."

I said to him, "Decker, is this the man (pointing to the officer) who arrested you?"

He answered, "Yes, sir"

I replied, "All right, Decker, keep quiet; we'll fix this!" and, stepping out into the street, it did not take me long to pick up a half dozen of our boys, who, marching to the hotel, I ordered them to march this *vulture* at the point of the bayonet up and down the street for half an hour.

It was a ludicrous scene, but richly enjoyed by many of the loyal citizens of that little town, and taught, at least one of these *sharks* that there is a wide difference between a sick comrade and a deserter.

I immediately sent Decker home again to his friends, where, I am sorry to say, the noble fellow died the following spring of consumption.

CHAPTER III.

Early in March, 1864, found us all in barracks at Flint, with over five hundred new recruits, one hundred of which were gathered from the northern towns of Livingston county.

Among the many was the Hon. Danford Parker of Osceola, since treasurer of that county.

Parker, when he enlisted, was one of the finest specimens of manhood, both physically and mentally, that could be found in that section of the country. He passed through the battles of the Wilderness, Spottsylvania, North Anna, Coal Harbor, and on to Petersburg with us, stacking his gun always with his company.

I never shall forget, when in front of Petersburg, he came to me the perfect picture of despair. I hardly knew him, he was so thin, for he could not have weighed much over a hundred pounds, the result of chronic diarrhea, contracted by exposure in the hard-fought battles through which he passed. I ordered him before an examining board, procured his discharge, handed him ten dollars, and told him to make tracks for home.

CHARLIE GARDNER,
Drummer Boy, 8th Michigan Infantry. Killed at Knoxville,
November 12, 1863.

Of that hundred men who enlisted, many of them are living today whose familiar forms flash before the mind's eye as I write these pages.

The citizens of Flint provided us with most excellent quarters, and contributed, as far as it was in their power, to make our stay pleasant, which they eminently succeeded in doing.

Colonel Fenton, then living, was the grand center of attraction to the older members of the regiment, and exerted himself in every way possible to secure our comfort and pleasure during our brief visit.

I never shall forget an interview with Mrs. Gardner, the mother of our drummer-boy Charlie, whom we lost at Knoxville. It seemed as though that mother's heart would break as she talked to me about her boy and the losses she had sustained by the terrible rebellion. Such interviews with friends and relatives of comrades we had left behind in unmarked graves at Flowerdale, Jackson, Blue Springs, Campbell Station and Knoxville were almost of hourly occurrence, and excited our deepest sympathy.

When we left Flint to return to the front we were under orders to rejoin the corps in Tennessee.

When we reached Louisville, Ky., the order

was countermanded, directing us to report at Annapolis, Md., where we arrived, via the Pennsylvania Central railroad, and steamed down Chesapeake Bay, reaching Annapolis about the middle of March, 1864.

We were encamped in barracks and tents just out of the city, and soon all the division of the corps began to arrive, making our numbers swell from an insignificant force to an army of forty thousand men, under the command of Major-General Burnside.

It was thought by some we were assembled there to make another expedition down the Atlantic coast, but General Grant had now been made Lieutenant-General of the Army, and we soon found out, if we had never known it before, that soldiers were machines moved by powers unseen.

Grant (that silent man) came and reviewed us sometime in April, and, knowing the good fighting material of which we were composed, ordered us to report early in May for duty with our old friends and comrades of the Army of the Potomac.

While we were at Annapolis a large number of cases of measles occurred throughout the corps, which the new recruits did not escape.

Our mortality was but slight, losing but three or four, two of whom, I remember—George Griswold of Company B, and Dwight Skinner of Company A.

We had no chaplain, and the boys, never liking the idea (if it were in any way possible to avoid it) of rolling their comrades into a hole like a dead dog, requested me to officiate. So I accompanied the funeral escort of my old neighbor to his last resting-place, and offered a few appropriate remarks, after which the sergeant in charge ordered the usual military salute, and we returned to our camp feeling sad at the thought that another of our brave comrades had gone to that "bourne from whence no traveler returns."

Skinner did not die until after we left Annapolis, where I left him in Navy Yard Hospital in charge of a lady of the Christian Commission, with the promise from her that he should receive every care possible, and if he died, she would immediately communicate with me and his family, whose address I furnished.

Those boys sleep today at Annapolis, their graves marked with suitable iron headboards furnished by the United States of America. They were both married men, and left widows and children now residing in this section of the country.

It will be remembered by comrades of the 8th that Captain R. N. Doyle had been put out of fight for many months, and that it was at this time he returned to us, having suffered from an ugly wound received at James Island (the excision of an elbow joint), and had languished in hospitals, a great sufferer from the time he left the regiment up to now.

His wound had in no wise healed, and unless he submitted to another painful operation he was informed it would be useless for him to attempt to enter into active service. He readily submitted to another operation, and I am glad to say the result was deeply gratifying.

Captain Doyle, who afterwards became lieutenant-colonel of the regiment, and commanded it in front of Petersburgh, was a brave and accomplished officer, a former resident of Grand Rapids, but now residing in California.

Colonel Ralph Ely having been assigned to the command of the second brigade of the division has become illustrious from the fact that his brigade was the first that entered Petersburgh upon the evacuation of Lee.

At the conclusion of the war Colonel Ely,

COL. RALPH ELY,
8th Michigan Infantry.

with the rank of brigadier, which he had richly earned, was placed in command of a district in South Carolina, as superintendent under General O. O. Howard.

The regiment was greatly attached to Colonel Ely, who was always a brave, generous, and kind-hearted gentleman, and under any circumstances, no matter how afflicted himself, he never forgot his men, but exerted himself to the utmost to make us as comfortable as circumstances would permit.

After the close of the war he was twice auditor general of the State, discharging his duties with great credit, and died a few years ago in the village of Ely, named after him, in Emmet county, this State, Michigan.

> Rest, noble warrior, rest.
> Your duties well performed:
> You led us on to victory,
> No matter what the storm.

The time spent at Annapolis was improved in the drilling of our new recruits and bringing all the departments to the highest state of efficiency. Daily dress parades were held, all insubordination was quickly noticed and punished—if necessary—instantly. The colonel being determined his regiment should compare favorably with, if not excel in discipline, any of the other regiments of the division. He issued almost daily some sort of special order to achieve this result; so much so, in fact, that the boys used to say "the Colonel had a perfect diarrhea of orders."

We took up our march on the 23d day of April, 1864, passing through Washington, President Lincoln reviewing us, the boys giving him three times three and a tiger as they passed down on to Long Bridge, and back into Virginia, to complete the unfinished work of subjugating the most terrible rebellion recorded in the annals of history today.

We encamped that night back of Alexandria, Va., where we remained two days, and resumed our march on the 26th, by way of Fairfax, Centreville, on to Warrenton Station, where we remained until the 2d of May. Several cases of smallpox occurring among the recruits at this point, they were placed in quarters remote from the command and returned to the pest hospital, at an early date, in the rear of Alexandria.

At this point I advised one of our best officers, Captain John C. Buchannan, who had been suffering from ill health for many months and was utterly unable, however much he desired to continue with us, to resign, which he did, and I am happy to say the advice was timely, he having, to a great extent, regained his health, and is now a very valued citizen of Grand Rapids, Mich.

On the morning of the 4th of May we resumed our march by way of Rappahannock Station, where we encamped for the night, and on the morning of the 5th proceeded by rapid marching and crossed the Rapidan at Germania Ford.

A few miles before we reached the Ford we crossed a small stream, and Colonel Frank Graves, commanding the regiment, undertook to ride across a mill dam, just below where the boys forded the stream, but his horse's feet slipping both horse and rider were submerged in the muddy water. Even though the men may have largely sympathized with the colonel in his mishap, they could not possibly refrain from indulging in a shout of laughter at his ludicrous appearance. The colonel's baggage being well to the rear, and mine, as it usually was, well up, I soon made our colonel presentable again in my own wardrobe.

Of course some delay was occasioned by this, so that the troops got somewhat in advance. I remember saying to him:

"Colonel, if a Roman had suffered your mishap he would consider it as a forewarning of his downfall in battle."

We went into camp that evening on Wilderness Run. The main body of the Army of the Potomac wènt across the night before, and had already engaged the enemy.

Sedgwick, Hancock, Warren and Sheridan on our side, and Lee with his army were hotly engaged. I think I never heard such musketry firing as occurred all along the line that night.

It was plain to be seen that on the sixth there was a hot day's work before us.

We were advanced to the front quite early, being about the center of Grant's army. Our Division Hospital, in charge of Surgeon Bonine of the 2d Michigan, was established near Wilderness Run, in order that we might obtain sufficient water, and care well for our wounded.

Our corps charged the center of the enemy's line not far from noon that day, and met a terrible reverse. It is said by men present on the field that Colonel Graves was taken prisoner, and that his captors immediately shot him down and stripped him of all clothing. There is, undoubtedly, much truth in the report, for we never succeeded in recovering his body. His father, a resident of Niles, Michigan, visited us later on, but no traces of our colonel could be found.

Colonel Frank Graves was a graduate of West Point, and was made lieutenant-colonel upon the first organization of the regiment. He was a very fine, cultured, military gentleman, social to a degree, pleasant, but a thorough disciplinarian.

Could he have been spared longer to the service of his country there is no doubt but what he would have risen rapidly.

The following are the names of the wounded brought to the Division Field Hospital, including those of all the Michigan troops in our division :

BATTLE OF THE WILDERNESS, MAY 6, 1864.

Name.	Rank.	Co.	Regiment.	Missile.	Nature of Wound.
Vaughn, B. F.	Cor.	C	17th Mich.	Shell.	Neck, contusion, slight, simple dressing.
Herrick, Nelson	Pr.	I	27th "	Ball.	Right side, flesh, accidental, simple.
Scott, Ezra S.	Cor.	D	1st Mich. S. S.	"	Shoulder blade, with fracture.
Allen, Charles	1st Sergt.	K	" "	"	Left side.
Caddy, Thomas	Pr.	F	27th Mich.	"	Left wrist, flesh, simple dressing.
Palmer, Stewart	Cor.	B	2d "	"	Left small finger, severe, amputated.
Bywater, Abel	Pr.	H	8th "	"	Head, entered left cheek near angle of nose, exit neck behind left ear, also slight flesh wound right tibia.
Barden, S. C.	Capt.	B	2d "	"	Right thumb, amputated.
Crozier, James	Sergt.	A	27th "	"	Right ear, cutting flesh behind and before the ear, carrying away lower front teeth.
Fancet, Robert	Pr.	B	8th "	"	Left hand, second finger amputated.
Clark, William A.	1st Sergt.	H	" "	"	Mouth, lower front teeth and alveola removed.
Joss, John C.	1st Lieut.	G	2d "	"	Left knee joint, amputated.
Van Valkenburg, R. T.	Pr.	A	17th "	"	Right hand and fingers, amputated.
Whiting, Thos. J.	Sgt. Maj.	I	2d "	"	Left leg, fracture of tibia and fibula, amputated leg and third and small fingers.
Donahue, James S.	Capt.	A	8th "	"	Fracture left femur, amputated middle third thigh.
Apanna, Rob.	Pr.	I	27th "	"	Left elbow joint, amputated above elbow.
Coleman, Wm.	Cor.	D	17th "	"	Humerus fracture, amputated upper third.
Kelsch, Ellsha	Pr.	D	8th "	"	Right thigh, flesh, simple dressing.

Name	Rank	Co.	Regiment		Wound
Hall, Cyrus W.	Cor.	G	1st Mich. S.S.	"	Abdomen, entered near umbilicus; died May 7, 1864.
Chapman, C. F.	Pr.	F	2d	"	Abdomen, left umbilicus; died May 7, 1864.
Shull, Ed.	"	K	"	"	Abdomen, left umbilicus, entered near spine.
Atwood, Chas.	"	I	"	"	Back, entered near spine, passing in chest.
Hovey, Edwin	1st Lieut.	B	8th	"	Left thigh and left leg, flesh, simple dressing.
Fifield Paul	Pr.	K	27th	"	Both femurs fractured, simple dressing, splint.
Thayer, Frank	"	"	8th	"	Point of the shoulder and arm, penetrated capulis, lower edge of scapula broken off, remove fragment, simple dressing.
Chamberlain, S.	"	D	"	"	Right elbow joint, severe, amputated lower third.
Mullin, Chas.	"	E	27th	"	Right cheek, flesh, simple dressing.
Taylor, George	"	D	8th	"	Thigh, lower third, flesh.
Ganso, Theo.	"	G	"	"	Left hip, flesh.
Lester, Westover	"	F	27th	"	Second left hand, flesh.
Downing, John	"	K	8th	"	Right arm.
Foldner, Joseph	"	A	27th	"	Right arm.
Hibbard, Chas.	"	G	8th	"	Left shoulder, flesh.
Hammond, Chas.	"	C	27th	"	Forehead, slight, flesh.
Barker, Truman	"	H	2d	"	Right forearm fractured, slight.
Smith, Jerome	"	D	27th	"	Penetrated chest; died May 7, 1864.
Weller, William	"	K	8th	"	Right arm, flesh.
White, Wesley L.	"	D	8th	"	Right hip, flesh.
Chipadore, Andr.	"	B	17th	"	Abdomen, found dead on street, name on badge.

BATTLE OF THE WILDERNESS.—Continued.

Name.	Rank.	Co.	Regiment.	Missile.	Nature of Wound.
Douglass, George	Pr.	B	17th Mich.	Ball.	Left ankle joint, ball extracted.
Grotenhuse, James	"	D	8th "	"	Tibia and fibula fractured.
O'Callahan, J.	"	G	17th "	"	Humerus fractured, amputated upper third, left ankle.
Wilson, John	Cor.	E	27th "	"	Heel.
Adair	Pr.	A	8th "	"	Right shoulder.
Atherton, John J.	"	"	" "	"	Right arm, flesh.
Passage, Jacob	Cor.	I	27th "	"	Right lower maxillary and right shoulder.
Babcock, Dwight	Pr.	H	" "	"	Left shoulder.
Inglebeart, Fredk	"	A	" "	"	Right foot.
Ellis, Gilbert	"	K	" "	"	Right cheek.
Twist, Theo. H.	"	"	" "	"	Left arm, flesh, slight.
Van Dusen, Ch.	Cor.	I	" "	"	Right arm.
Perkins, Homer	Pr.	1 s. s.	" "	"	Left finger, flesh.
Leeman, Wm.	"	F	8th "	"	Right cheek, flesh.
Blood, Albt.	"	E	" "	"	Left elbow, flesh.
Wilber, Palmer H.	"	I	27th "	"	Right ear.
Marshall, Samuel H.	"	"	" "	"	Left thumb.
Kershaw, Francis	"	2 s. s.	" "	"	Right side and hand, flesh.

Name	Rank	Co.	Regt.		Wound
Sonanger, Stephen	Sergt.	E	"	"	Left knee, flesh.
Clark, Edgar J	Pr.	I	8th "	"	Left ankle, flesh.
Hollenback, J	Cor.	"	"	"	Right elbow.
McKay, Chris	Pr.	A	27th "	"	Right leg fractured and left fingers.
Stringham, Dan. H	"	E	"	"	Right thigh, flesh.
Colvin, Stephen G	"	I	2d "	"	Back.
Stephenson, Thos. W	"	E	"	"	Left breast; dead.
Burroughs, Wm	"	C	1st Mich. S. S.	"	Left foot, flesh, slight.
Bigelow, David	"	F	2d Mich.	"	Humerus fractured, amputated.
Goodluck, Wm	Cor.	"	8th "	"	Left groin.
Brott, Chas	Pr.	E	"	"	Left small toe.
Cline, Mark	"	"	8th "	"	Right shoulder, flesh.
Van Ry, Frank	"	D	"	"	Forehead, slight.
Hickman, Clement	Sergt.	C	"	"	Scalp, slight.
Minacke, Fredk	Pr.	"	"	"	Chest.
Schwartz, Fred	"	B	"	"	Left middle finger.
Remmell, B. S	"	H	1st Mich. S. S.	"	Left shoulder.
Skinner, Eugene	"	C	"	"	Left side, flesh.
Doolittle, Lucky	"	"	8th Mich.	"	Right leg.
Taylor, George	"	D	"	"	Right thigh, flesh.
Burbank, G. W	Cor.	C	"	"	Right leg fractured.

BATTLE OF THE WILDERNESS.—*Continued.*

Name.	Rank.	Co.	Regiment.	Missile.	Nature of Wound.
Dickerman, J.	Sergt.	C	8th Mich	Ball.	Right leg fractured.
Woodhead, W. S.	Pr.	G	2d "	"	Scalp, flesh.
Sowles, J. H.	"	A	1st Mich. S. S.	"	Neck, left side.
Acker, C. T.	Sergt.	I	20th Mich.	"	Left little toe.
Semkout, Wm.	"	D	17th "	"	Side, contusion.
Frost, David	Pr.	B	8th "	"	Left little finger.
Gage, Wm. M.	Cor.	G	" "	"	Excision of left shoulder joint.
Rayner, Wm.	"	A	20th "	"	Left shoulder.
Kenyon, Avery	Pr.	I	27th "	"	Head; died in ambulance May 6, 1864.
Wilson, Robert	"	F	" "	"	Left hand, slight.
Smith, Gil.	Cor.	D	17th "	"	Back, slight.
Willetts, Sam.	Pr.	G	" "	"	Left hand and wrist.
Gregory, J. B.	Cor.	"	" "	"	Right arm flesh.
Hanchett, C. H.	Pr.	"	" "	"	Right thumb and left hand.
Frost, Ira	"	H	" "	"	Right little finger.
Calf, James	"	C	" "	"	Right shoulder.
Hague, Edwin	Sergt.	G	17th "	"	Right knee.
Drake, Wm. P.	"	H	27th "	"	Left hand.

FRANK GLEASON,
Co. B., 8th Michigan Infantry. Twice wounded, and prisoner of war at Andersonville, Ga.

Name	Rank	Co.	Regt.	Wound
Dudley, Ed. R.	Pr.	G	17th Mich.	Left second and third fingers.
Wing, Warner	"	H	8th "	Right arm and elbow.
Drury, G. H.	"	A	" "	Fourth left toe, slight.
Shepard, Irwin	Cor.	E	17th "	Left shoulder, fracture.
Coles, C. D.	"	D	" "	Left arm, flesh.
Powell, A. F.	"	"	" "	Right shoulder.
Hoover, Franklin	"	"	27th "	Right thumb, flesh.
Evers, G. M.	Sergt.	"	17th "	Left thigh, flesh; shoulder, slight.
Smith, Gilbert	Cor.	D	" "	Both shoulders, flesh.
Bist, John	Pr.	A	" "	Left shoulder, flesh.
Rector, W. W.	"	D	" "	Right shoulder, flesh.
Diltz, H.	"	I	" "	Left foot, slight.
Miller, R. B.	"	A	" "	Right shoulder, flesh.
Fountain, Phil.	"	G	" "	Left arm, slight flesh.
Smith, Fran.	"	B	" "	Back of neck, flesh.
Willetts, Jos. W.	Cor.	A	" "	Right arm fractured, arm amputated middle third.
Church, G. C.	Pr.	"	" "	Scalp, slight.
Mapes, Lawrence	"	"	" "	Back, flesh.
Baldwin, M.	"	"	" "	Knee contusion, slight.
Kelly, Thomas	"	"	" "	Left arm, flesh.
Gleason, F. G.	Sergt.	B	8th "	Prisoner six months; wound, middle third right leg fracture.

BATTLE OF THE WILDERNESS.—*Continued.*

Name.	Rank.	Co.	Regiment.	Missile.	Nature of Wound.
Dolph, Simeon	Pr.	B	8th Mich.	Ball.	Died at Andersonville, August, 1864.
Wychoff, J. R.	"	"	"	"	Injured by ambulance, May 6, 1864.
Moshler, G.	"	"	"	"	Left hand.
Pellett, W.	"	F	"	"	Dislocation of patella and fracture of knee.
Doane, J. W.	Lieut.	C	"	"	Left knee.
Niland, Henry	Pr.	D	"	"	Died at Andersonville, September, 1864; scurvy.

The 8th Infantry went into the Battle of the Wilderness about nine hundred strong, but when they came out the roll call accounted for about four hundred men. Having lost their colonel, four line officers wounded, and Captain Hutchinson of Company B taken prisoner.

Captain Hutchinson was confined in Danville military prison until some time in the winter of 1864-5. He was a truly brave man; too brave for his own good, for there are times in a military man's life when caution is necessary.

After his parole he returned to St. Johns, this State (Mich.), where he died soon after of dementia (a disease of the brain) brought about by the extreme privations of the military prison.

Captain Hutchinson left a wife and, I think, one daughter. I remember Mrs. Hutchinson was offered a position in the auditor general's office during the incumbency of Colonel Ralph Ely, who, upon the death of General Graves, took command of the old 8th, and was in command of the brigade when it occupied Petersburgh on the retreat of Lee. It is a matter of public record in the archives of the State that Mrs. Hutchinson was a very accomplished lady, and filled her position very satisfactorily.

Late on the night of the 7th the Army of the

Potomac commenced swinging its right towards Spottsylvania, and Sedgwick's Vermonters passing our hospital, gave our surgeon-in-chief, Dr. Bonine, some anxiety lest we should have to leave some of our wounded. But the old surgeon had his eye open, and when his boys were concerned there was but a very little of any importance that escaped him. So, our hospital was soon loaded up and all of the wounded were soon on their way to Chancellorsville, which point we reached the next afternoon, where fully twelve thousand wounded were concentrated.

About dark I received an order from the medical director of the army to proceed with the train to Fredericksburg, and there make them as comfortable as possible, informing me that stores had already arrived there. I was also directed to complete what operations had been overlooked.

I remember, and it doubtless is vividly borne in mind by many of the wounded of that train, the sufferings endured by them as we wound along our weary journey from Chancellorsville to Fredericksburg, stopping to bury our dead nearly every mile along that memorable road.

A wounded man, from loss of blood, suffers greatly from thirst, and it was no uncommon

FREDERICKSBURG, VA., 1864.

thing, as I rode up and down that line, to hear the boys cry out, "For God's sake, doctor, give us some water!"

We obtained all we could from wells, cisterns and pools along our route, and distributed it as impartially as possible under the circumstances.

Some, undoubtedly, died of thirst, but the majority met their death from the reaction and shock which always occurs to badly wounded men.

The 24th New York Cavalry preceded my train as escort. As we neared Fredericksburg, it was rumored among them that the city was occupied by the enemy, and it was not safe to proceed. I felt positive the medical authorities would not have ordered that train into the camp of an enemy, so I thought it advisable to proceed as fast as possible.

I had a hospital guard, composed of fifty of the 51st Pennsylvania, who I asked to drive the cavalry off the pike to allow us to continue our journey, that we might get where we could obtain water and comfort for those suffering heroes.

The 51st, like the 79th, had had many experiences together with us, and knew full well that they would not be asked to discharge a duty without a reasonable expectation of safe results.

That 24th soon *skedaddled*, and left the way open, and we saw nothing of them until after we arrived at Fredericksburg and had our wounded all cared for. This did not take long, because under such circumstances we were not very particular what we seized that would contribute to the comfort of our boys.

The Planters' Hotel, churches, schools, houses, and even Mayor Slaughter's house, were confiscated for the benefit of our suffering comrades (and there was a considerable number of them), there being six Michigan regiments in the division at that time—the 2d, 8th, 17th, 20th, 27th, and the 1st Michigan Sharpshooters.

CAPTAIN J. S. DONAHUE,
8th Michigan Infantry.

CHAPTER IV.

At the terrible battle of the 6th of May, 1864, among the more prominent officers of the 8th not before alluded to, was Captain James S Donahue, Company A, now in charge of the lighthouse service on Lake Michigan.

Captain Donahue had been severely wounded at James Island, South Carolina, by a shell, and now lost his left leg, being compelled to have it amputated above the knee. He was idolized by his men, and was ever thoughtful of their comfort in camp, and no sacrifice was too great for him if leading a forlorn hope.

Lieutenant Edwin M. Hovey, of Company B, also received a severe wound, and I am happy to say, that both he and Captain Donahue have recovered so as to pursue a more peaceable avocation in the future.

As soon as the wounded were made comfortable in Fredericksburg the medical officers immediately returned to the front, where we found severe fighting at Spottsylvania.

Our field hospital was located at what was then known as the "Harris House," one of those old Virginia homes surrounded by commodious porches so well appreciated in the South, with their slave quarters in the rear, standing about a mile and a half in the rear of the line of battle. Our stretcher bearers and ambulance corps were kept busy day and night bringing in the wounded.

The casualties of the 8th at Spottsylvania were not equal to those of the Wilderness. Farma, a private of E; Rollo, sergeant of H; Kilburn of C; McLaughlin, sergeant of I; John N. Stewart of C; Lieutenant J. A. Elder of E; Coffee of F; Capt. C. F. Smith of C; Chamberlain of D; Loomis of H; Green of B; Sawyer of G; Scott of K; Cornell of E, seems to cover our list of casualties.

The army lost at the battle of Spottsylvania, according to official reports, 4,177 in killed, and 19,687 in wounded.

Among the illustrious names I now remember I find Sedgwick, Crittenden, well-known to fame and the color-bearers of the 8th and 79th. And when Morrison exclaimed, "Come, First Brigade, carry those works!" they shook out their colors and the whole command started on the double-quick until the gallant Morrison received an ugly wound which shattered his right hand, sending him to the rear. But Lang, Gair and Baird

CAPTAIN JOHN A. ELDER,
8th Michigan Infantry.

of the 79th had so far escaped. Ely, Lewis and Belcher of the 8th still held on, rebuilt our works and saved the line.

Three days hard fighting since the battle of the Wilderness had now occurred, and Grant wrote his ever-memorable letter to the President

"I will fight it out on this line if it takes all summer, and if I am not through then will get a stove."

I was at the "Harris House" at this time, caring for the men who had performed such heroic deeds. As soon as possible all the wounded were shipped to Fredericksburg under my immediate supervision, and shipped, as fast as steamers could be obtained, to Northern hospitals. A large percentage were so badly wounded they were unable to report for duty again.

A few years ago the adjutant general of the army, by special order, directed all surgeons having important records in their possession to forward them to Washington, with which I, of course, complied, and imagine my chagrin upon the return of the books to find one, covering our operations in East Tennessee and recording the sick and wounded, missing. The only satisfaction I obtained was a note to the effect that the book was too valuable a compilation of facts to exist outside of the bureau of the army to which it related.

This seems to me a very strange proceeding, as I had ever complied with the Articles of War in making regular monthly returns to the surgeon-general of all that occurred relating to the army. Could I have retained that volume many men, women and orphans of deceased comrades would have obtained what the Government promised them when they entered the service.

After our return from Fredericksburg we found the army had made another flank movement, attempting to cross the North Anna, which Hampton and Stuart were bound to defeat. But, lucky for us, Sheridan and Meade a few days before, had some sharp words at Spottsylvania.

My idea of Sheridan (which was, to a large extent, indorsed by many other officers), was, that he was a sort of Ney.

General Meade was a nice sort of gentleman, who understood the art of war as taught by logarithms and abtruse engineering. That sort of business may have answered the purpose some centuries ago, but a new era had dawned in the art of war which had taught us a lesson which, no doubt, will ever be followed by contending armies in the future. Heretofore the cavalry arm of the service had simply escorted headquarters and guarded the flanks of the army. Sheridan did not believe in that doctrine. He maintained, in a sharp encounter with Meade, that the cavalry should be an independent command, and if he would allow him, he would take care of Stuart so that the infantry could take care of themselves. The cavalry were usually regarded by the infantry as an obstruction, while on the march, rather than of service.

The pontoon bridges, on our arrival, were quickly under a galling fire from Breckenridge's corps, but that did not stop the six Michigan regiments, under General O. B. Wilcox, from carrying the point and driving the rebels back, enabling us to establish our line on the Richmond side of that river.

Hancock, of the Second Corps, and Warren, of the Fifth, were equally vigilant at different points along the line, and on the morning of the 25th of May our lines were secure where the general-in-chief designed to place them.

The following are the names of the wounded at the

BATTLE OF SPOTTSYLVANIA.

Name.	Rank.	Co.	Regiment.	Missile.	Nature of Wound.
Laboran, Frank	Musen.	K	20th Mich.	Ball.	Left arm, amputated middle third.
O'Leary, Jere.	Cor.	H	1st Mich. S. S.	"	Scalp, flesh.
Ash, David	Pr.	G	"	"	Right breast and arm, slight.
Brewer, J. H.	"	D	"	"	Left shoulder and cheek.
Doty, L. L.	"	I	20th Mich.	"	Left thigh, flesh.
Lawrence, M. J.	"	"	"	"	Left wrist, flesh.
Miller, Wm.	"	"	"	"	Left thigh, flesh.
Barnhart, Ja.	Cor.	E	1st Mich. S. S.	"	Left hand, second finger.
Farms, Heidrick	Pr.	"	8th "	"	Right forefinger, amputated.
Heggleton, Oliver	"	D	1st Mich. S. S.	"	Left arm, contusion, slight.
Benedict, J. A.	"	"	"	"	Spine.
Crater, Barney	Cor.	H	"	"	Forehead over right eye, slight.
Fansler, G.	Pr.	C	"	"	Left forearm, flesh.
Andress, E. V.	Capt.	K	"	"	Right foot, slight.
Quance, Stephen	Pr.	H	"	"	Head and left temple.
Jackson, John	"	E	"	"	Left hip, flesh.
Livingstone, John	"	A	"	"	Right foot, amputated.
Hinkley, Ben. F.	"	"	"	"	Left arm, flesh.

Name	Rank	Co.	Regiment		Wound
Perry, Oliver E.		B	"	"	Head, occipital protuberance.
Fountains, Foslans	"	F	"	"	Left hand, flesh.
Woods, Wm.	"	D	"	"	Left foot.
Hart, Andrew R.	"	"	"	"	Right temple.
McLoud, Dan.	"	A	"	"	Right breast, contusion.
Buchanan, Arthur	"	I	"	"	Back, entered between vertebra and scapula.
Smith, Henry	"	E	20th Mich.	"	Left hip, superficial.
Hathaway, Walter	"	H	1st Mich. S. S.	"	Abdomen, passing through mouth; died May 19, '64.
Thompson, Wm. J.	"	D	20th Mich.	"	Head, scalp wound above left ear.
West, George	"	I	1st Mich. S. S.	"	Left thigh, contusion.
Phelps, Melvin	Cor.	C	"	"	Head, flesh wound of scalp.
Palmer, Franklin	Pt.	B	"	"	Left leg, flesh wound.
Patterson, Henry	Sergt.	D	"	"	Right gluteal region.
Easy, John	"	A	"	"	Hip, flesh.
Sanders, John S.	"	"	"	"	Left hand.
Miller, A. M.	Cor.	K	"	"	Left shoulder, contusion.
Stoneman, Geo.	Pr.	A	"	"	Hand, second middle, fingers amputated.
Kimball, Otis	"	D	"	"	Right humerus fracture, amputated middle third.
Read, John	"	A	5th "	"	Left hip, flesh.
Reed, Alfred	"	I	27th "	"	Left forearm, flesh.
Decker, W. S.	"			"	Left hand, first two fingers.

BATTLE OF SPOTTSYLVANIA.—Continued.

Name.	Rank.	Co.	Regiment.	Missile.	Nature of Wound.
Cutcheon, B. M.	Cor.	I	20th Mich.	Ball.	Right and forearm.
Brambart, Mat.	Pr.	A	27th "	"	Ankle fracture, amputated below third of leg.
Munn, Wm.	"	"	" "	"	Head of humerus, excision.
Fishell, Albert	"	"	" "	"	No wound given.
Hunt, John	"	E	1st Mich. S. S.	"	No wound given.
Stevens, Aug.	"	A	20th Mich.	"	No wound given.
Beckwith, Silas	"	C	1st Mich. S. S.	"	No wound given.
Jack, Alex.	"	B	17th Mich.	"	Left shoulder, penetrated abdomen; died May 11, '64.
Farrell, Joseph	Sergt.	G	1st Mich. S. S.	"	Left forearm, flesh.
Secor, Henry	Cor.	I	" "	"	Right forearm, flesh.
Buckley, E. J.	Adj.	"	" "	Shell.	Scalp, flesh.
Hoffman, D. J.	Sergt.	A	20th Mich.	Ball.	Left great toe, flesh.
Vorhees, Abram	Pr.	I	" "	"	Metatarsal.
Thomas, A. P.	2d Lieut.	C	1st Mich. S. S.	"	Left foot.
Sturger, M. H.	Pr.	D	" "	"	Right arm.
Samore, John	"	A	27th Mich.	"	Right arm.
Robarge, G.	2d Lieut.	H	17th "	Shell.	Left leg, flesh.
Dago, John	Pr.	B	26th "	Ball.	Right forearm.

Name	Rank	Co.	Regt.		Cause	Description
Brinks, Bradley	"	G	20th	"		Left shoulder, ball not found.
Rollo, Albert	Sergt.	H	8th	"		Left shoulder, amputated head of scapula.
Willis, Geo.	Cor.	A	27th	"		Left thigh, flesh.
Danser, Leroy	Pr.	K	20th	"	Shell.	Shoulder, flesh contusion.
Allen, Oliver	"	"	"	"	"	Left cheek, slight.
Hill, Wallace	Cor.	A	27th	"	"	Right arm, contusion.
Pike, Murray	"	B	"	"	"	Left thumb.
Page, Ben	Pr.	I	"	"	"	Left hip, severe; died May 15, 1864.
Lehman, Fred	"	K	20th	"	"	Left thigh, contusion.
Sumner, Geo.	Cor.	"	27th	"	"	Left leg fractured, amputated upper third femur; died May 14, 1864.
Profser, John	Pr.	"	20th	"	"	Nates and back.
Stiles, G. W.	"	I	"	"	"	Left hand, flesh.
McKinsey, Dan.	"	K	"	"	"	Hip and heel, contusion.
Smith, James H.	"	K	27th	"	Ball.	Right leg, flesh.
Jeffries, Chas.	Sergt.	"	"	"	"	Left breast and lower maxillary.
Bone, Francis	Pr.	E	"	"	"	Left shoulder, laceration.
Blett, Nicholas	Cor.	A	27th	"	"	Left index finger.
Osel, Florin	Pr.	B	27th	"	"	Left elbow, contusion.
Myers, Henry	"	C	"	"	"	Left foot, flesh.
Seeley, Gilbert	"	D	"	"	"	Right shoulder, flesh.
Foster, Levi	"	"	"	"	"	Right heel.

BATTLE OF SPOTTSYLVANIA.—Continued.

Name.	Rank.	Co.	Regiment.	Missile.	*Nature of Wound.
Crothers, Wm	Pr.	C	27th Mich	Shell.	Head, skull fractured; died May 15, 1864.
Sheridan, James	"	B	" "	Ball.	Left hip, fracture; died May 14, 1864.
Chittyo, Thomas	Sergt.	K	1st Mich. S. S.	Shell.	Left forearm, fracture; died May 14, 1864.
Wallace, Alex	Pr.	"	" "	Ball.	Left wrist.
Behent, Valentine	"	"	27th Mich	Shell.	Right hand, index and second fingers.
Burke, Henry	"	K	" "	Ball.	Left hand, small finger.
Merrit, J. G.	"	B	17th "	"	Right arm, flesh.
Boylin, Chas	"	"	20th "	"	Nose, flesh, slight.
Allen, C. T.	Capt.	D	2d "	"	Left groin, slight.
Walker, A. W.	Pr.	"	20th "	"	Right hand and index finger, and thumb.
Weakly, John	"	K	1st Mich. S. S.	"	Left wrist.
Vallegmilt, Joe	"	F	17th Mich	"	Head.
Lemorand, Joe	"	C	8th "	"	Left shoulder.
Kilbourn, Lucien	"	S. S.	27th "	"	Right arm fractured, resection of humerus, upper third.
Dolph, Joseph	Sergt.	H	1st Mich. S. S.	"	Right hand, forefinger.
Beadle, Ed	Pr.	E	8th Mich	"	Right side.
Rosencranz, I. D.	Cor.	K	27th "	"	Right leg, fibula fractured.
Raynor, Ashen					Left knee.

THE GREAT REBELLION.

Name	Rank	Co.	Regt.		Description
Antis, Val	"	C	27th "	"	Neck.
Adams, Geo. H	Pr.	2 S. S.	"	"	Left arm.
Merritt, Ed	"	"	"	"	Left thigh, flesh.
Weller, Chas	"	C	17th "	"	Left thigh, flesh.
Ayers, Harrison	"	I	20th "	"	Left thigh and hip, ball exit.
Hosmer, Ben	Cor.	B	1st Mich	Ball.	Right shoulder.
Spindler, J	Pr.	E	27th "	"	Left shoulder.
Moore, James L	Sergt.	G	17th "	"	Right elbow.
Myer, John	Pr.	1 S. S.	27th "	"	Right foot.
Betts, Randolph	"	C	1st Mich. S. S.	"	Left knee; died May 14, 1864.
McLaughlin, L	Sergt.	"	8th Mich	"	Scalp.
Timminer, G	Pr.	D	20th "	"	Left hand, index finger.
Hubbell, N. T	"	H	27th "	"	Right hand thumb.
Mead, I. M	"	D	17th "	"	Left elbow.
Burr, G. W	"	"	20th "	"	Left hand fingers.
Genovo, Louis	"	K	1st "	"	Left leg, flesh.
Davis, C. E	"	I	20th "	"	Left hand, flesh.
Wens, Wm	"	B	1st "	"	Head, scalp wound.
Sonerant, Eli	"	G	17th "	"	Right shoulder, contusion.
Stewart, John	"	C	8th "	"	Right side.
Smith, W. A	Cor.	A	17th "	"	Right shoulder, contusion.

BATTLE OF SPOTTSYLVANIA.—Continued.

Name.	Rank.	Co.	Regiment.	Missile.	*Nature of Wound.
Smith, E. L.	Pr.	F	17th Mich.	Ball.	Lip, slight.
Potter, A. W.	"	K	27th "	"	Forearm.
Shroykert, Louis	"	C	27th "	"	Left shoulder.
Filch, Geo. B.	"	D	20th "	"	Right elbow.
Smith, W. H.	"	A	17th "	"	Left ankle.
Dredge, James	"	K	8th "	"	Left hand.
Biggins, Tho.	"	A	17th "	"	Left wrist, flesh.
Dumez, Garret	"	F	1st "	"	Right arm.
Wright, Clark	"	I	" "	"	Left hand.
Elder, J. A.	2d Lieut.	E	8th "	"	Right arm.
Farwell, E.	Pr.	A	1st Mich. S. S.	"	Left ear and neck.
Oswald, Henry	"	C	27th Mich.	"	Left hand fingers.
Campbell, J.	Cor.	D	" "	"	Left arm.
Sugmiller, Geo.	Sergt.	I S. S.	" "	"	Right forearm, near elbow.
Reynolds, Jere.	Pr.	F	" "	"	Thigh, severe; died May 16, 1864.
Peltier, John	"	D	" "	"	Right forearm.
Benton, Henry	"	H	20th "	"	Right hand, slight.
Moorhouse, Steph.	"	A	" "	"	Right elbow.

THE GREAT REBELLION. 79

Name	Rank	Co.	Regt.		Wound
Pierce, O. W.	Cor.	C	27th	"	Left elbow, contusion.
Rulison, G.	Sergt.	B	20th	"	Left arm, contusion.
Wise, John	Pr.	E	1st	"	Left leg and forearm.
Delong, John	"	B	"	"	Neck.
Paul, John	"	E	"	"	Left hand, second and third fingers.
Smith, Howard	"	D	27th	"	Right hand, flesh.
Parker, W. H.	Sergt.	D	20th	"	Right arm.
Betts, Wallace	Pr.	C	7th	"	Left forearm.
Hero, Wm.	"	F	"	"	Left shoulder.
Sheen, Tim	"	C	27th	"	Left side.
Mathews, John	Cor.	A	"	"	Left arm; died May 14, 1864.
Kearney, James	Sergt.	E	"	"	Left hand and forefinger.
Spaulding, Josiah	Cor.	K	17th	"	Left thigh, flesh.
Robinson, C. W.	Pr.	E	27th	"	Left temple, slight.
Barrett, Michael	"	G	20th	"	Right hand.
Foster, L. A.	"	B	"	"	Left shoulder.
Lyman, Astrant	"	K	1st	"	Back.
Briggs, Clark C.	"	D	20th	"	Abdomen, severe.
Adams, L. H.	"	C	1st	"	Left side.
Lazer, Webster E.	"	B	"	"	Right shoulder.
Hamley, Amos	"	D	"	"	Left shoulder.

BATTLE OF SPOTTSYLVANIA.—*Continued.*

Name.	Rank.	Co.	Regiment.	Missile.	Nature of Wound.
Knoll, John	Pr.	G	1st Mich.	Ball.	Right thigh, severe.
Phillips, Joe R.	"	C	2d "	"	Head.
Scoley, Lewis	"	E	20th "	"	Right forearm, flesh.
Drummond, Tim	"	F	27th "	"	Right hand, second and third fingers amputated.
Corcoran, John	"	K	" "	"	Head, scalp, flesh.
McGrath, James	"	E	" "	"	Head, flesh wound of scalp.
Schmoulder, Michael	"	H	" "	"	Left hand.
Phelps, Ezra	Sergt.	D	20th "	"	Back.
Fitzgeralds, John	Pr.	I	1st "	"	Right forearm.
Wagner, Will	"	C	" "	"	Right hand, thumb.
Bisboy, Jos.	"	H	27th "	"	Right hand, forefinger.
Rodgers, Theo.	"	D	20th "	"	Breast, slight.
Carr, Harvey	"	I	27th "	"	Left hand.
Snider, John	Sergt.	K	" "	"	Left hand, second finger.
Davis, Wm.	Pr.	A	1st "	"	Left thigh.
Egbert, W. F.	Cor.	H	27th "	"	Mouth and chin.
Barry, Geo.	"	D	" "	"	Lower jaw broken.
Maynard, W. S.	Pr.	D	20th "	"	Left forearm, flesh.

THE GREAT REBELLION.

Name	Rank	Co.	Regt.		Cause	Wound
Coffee, Patrick	"	F	8th "		"	Left arm, flesh, slight.
Arnold, Lewis	"	B	17th "		"	Left wrist, fracture.
Taladox, Thom	"	C	1st Mich. S. S.		"	Left shoulder.
Lovejoy, Hiram	"	A	20th "		"	Lips, slight.
Tabor, Joe	"	H	27th "		"	Right hand and thigh.
Broderick, Den	"	G	" "		"	Left knee.
Cantwell, Tho	"	H	27th "		Shell.	Shoulder.
Markle, David	Pr.	K	20th "		"	Left elbow and shoulder.
Craven, Matt	Cor.	F	27th "		"	Left hips.
Lebute, Alex	Pr.	B	" "		"	Right shoulder.
Burnett, Hezekiah	Muscn.		" "		"	Left breast.
Runnels, James	Pr.	E	27th "		Ball.	Right shoulder and upper lip, resection of upper third humerus.
Hollingshead, E	"	B	20th "		"	Left hand and arm.
Marks, James	"	K	27th "		"	Right side and back.
Klinck, Jacob	"	A	2d "		Shell.	Shoulder, contusion.
Tolles, Seth H	"	E	16th "		Ball.	Head, scalp, slight.
Claborne, R	"	I	27th "		"	Right shoulder.
Smith, C. F	Capt.	C	8th "		"	Left hip.
Putman, H	Cor.	I	27th "		"	Left hand.
Twick, G. F	Sergt.	A	" "		"	Left side and shoulder.
Green, Harmon F	Pr.	E	" "		"	Head, slight.

BATTLE OF SPOTTSYLVANIA.—Continued.

Name.	Rank.	Co.	Regiment.	Missile.	Nature of Wound.
Brown, Fred	Pr.	B	17th Mich.	Ball.	Left wrist.
Zayer, Jacob	"	F	20th "	"	Left leg.
Campbell, B. H.	"	D	" "	Shell.	Left hip.
Mocurimund, D.	"	K	1st Mich. S. S.	Ball.	Left hand, right arm, and face.
Fleming, R.	"	E	17th "	"	Right side.
Field, Irwin	"	F	20th "	"	Nose.
Lounsberry, C. O.	1st Lieut.	I	" "	"	Left leg.
Smalley, M. C.	Pr.	D	27th "	"	Right shoulder, flesh, slight.
Swift, Frank	"	C	8th "	"	Left leg.
Clement, Lewis	1st Sergt.	H	27th "	"	Right shoulder and chest.
Shedoxe, Joe	Pr.	A	1st Mich. S. S.	"	Left hand, index finger.
McCarthy, Nelson	"	H	27th "	"	Left hip.
Sanez, Wellington	"	I	20th "	"	Left knee.
McMaggoo, Geo.	"	K	1st Mich. S. S.	"	Left hand, amputation third finger.
Johnson, Isaac	Sergt.	A	27th "	"	Right hip.
George, David	Pr.	K	1st Mich. S. S.	"	Head.
Bowers, Lewis	"	F	20th "	"	Throat.
Armour, John	2d Lieut.	K	27th "	"	Breast.

THE GREAT REBELLION.   83

Name	Rank	Co.	Regt.		Wound
Mutton, Wm	"	F	20th	"	Right side and arm, slight.
Touence, Loren	"	G	17th	"	Nose and left side of face.
Moynahan, J	Sergt.	C	27th	"	Right shoulder.
Hulce, John	Pr.	"	20th	"	Breast.
Show-na-sunk, J	"	K	1st Mich. S. S.	"	Left leg.
Fishke, Nippe	"	"	"	"	Shoulder.
Orent, John	"	C	27th	"	Both cheeks—through.
Dally, Geo	1st Sergt.	H	17th	"	Right shoulder and chest, severe; died May 16, '64.
Chamberlain, G	Pr.	D	8th	"	Left knee joint fractured; amputated middle third thigh.
Gressagold, Simon	"	K	1st Mich. S. S.	"	Left side, severe.
Lomis, Monroe	"	H	8th	"	Left leg, flesh.
Green, M. D	"	B	8th	"	Hip, penetrating cavity abdomen; died May 15, '64.
Percival, Wm	"	F	27th	"	Left foot, contusion.
Ely, W. W	"	I	20th	"	Left leg.
Wilkins, Cha	Cor.	B	27th	"	Left thigh, flesh.
Sayer, Alb	Pr.	G	8th	"	Left thigh, severe.
Holmes, Tho	"	D	1st Mich. S. S.	"	Lift thigh, severe.
Monroe. Fr	"	H	17th	"	Left hip.
Doran, James	"	2 S. S.	27th	"	Left hand, index and second fingers.
Scott, Abram	"	K	8th	"	Left thigh, contusion.
Harper, Sam	"	A	1st Mich. S. S.	"	Right forearm, fracture; amputated middle third.

BATTLE OF SPOTTSYLVANIA.—Continued.

Name.	Rank.	Co.	Regiment.	Missile.	Nature of Wound.
Esson, H. J.	Pr.	G	17th Mich.	Ball.	Right leg, amputated.
Foulk, Levi	"	C	1st Mich. S. S.	"	Right foot, contusion.

SHARP SHOOTERS CASUALTIES.

Name.	Rank.	Co.	Regiment.	Missile	Nature of Wound.
May 14, 1864.					
Cummings, Robt.	Pr.	C	1st Mich. S.S.	Ball.	Right hand, second finger.
May 15, 1864.					
Glimps, John	"	I S.S.	27th "	"	Right foot.
Keneben, Wm.	"	F	"	"	Right shoulder.
Collar, Martin	"	H	"	"	Right arm, flesh.
Rose, Aaron	"	"	"	"	Right arm paralyzed by ball.
Hannibal, Chas.	"	D	"	"	Right hand, flesh.
May 17, 1864.					
Hernden, W. C.	"	D	27th "	"	Right ankle.
May 18, 1864.					
Missip, Ed.	"	K	1st Mich. S.S.	"	Right hand, flesh.
Perkins, Chas.	Capt.	F	27th Mich.	"	Left shoulder and breast.
Belvey, Henry	Pr.	D	"	"	Right arm, flesh.
May 20, 1864.					
Cornell, Philo	"	E	8th "	"	Abdomen, mortal; died May 20, 1864.

NORTH ANNA.

There was no general engagement at North Anna, but our videts at the front kept up a constant fire with the enemy. The names of Michigan troops brought to the field hospital at that point are as follows:

Names.	Rank.	Co.	Regiment.	Missile.	Nature of Wound.
May 24, 1864.					
Howers, E. W.	Pr.	E	8th Mich.	Ball.	Right foot, accidental; amputated at ankle.
Campbell, C.	Sergt.	A	27th "	"	Right shoulder, flesh.
Sanderson, F.	Pr.	K	" "	"	Index finger; amputated fingers.
Wintersteen	"	H	" "	"	Left arm and flesh.
Horton, Hiram	"	"	" "	"	Left hand.
Flunkey, John	"	E	" "	"	Left arm, penetrating.
Fletcher, Nelson	2d Lieut.		2d "		Abdomen; brought dead to hospital.
Packard, Harry	Pr.	B	20th "	"	Lower lip.
Eastman, Emor.	"	2 S. S.	27th "	"	Neck, severe.
Davis, Sam	"	I	" "	"	Left leg.
Houghton, David	"	F	8th "	"	Left thumb, flesh.
May 25, 1864.					
Upham, Hiram	"	"	1st Mich. S. S.	"	Head, scalp wound.

THE GREAT REBELLION.

Name	Rank	Co.	Regiment		Injury
Shaw, Ed............	"	"	"	:	Right shoulder, slight contusion.
Fisher, Dan..........	"	A	"	:	Left elbow, flesh.
Tripp, Joes..........	"	"	"	:	Right leg, fractured; amputated upper third.
Baker, Jacob.........	"	H	2d Mich......	:	Head, mortal; died May 25, 1864.
Finch, Robt..........	"	B	1st Mich. S. S.	:	Head, skull fractured; pieces of bone removed and elevated.
Manchester, Perry....	"	C	20th "	:	Left leg, slight contusion.
May 28, 1864.					
Storr, George........	"	G	"	:	Right shoulder, exit between floating ribs, opposite side; died May 26, 1864.
Call, Augustus.......	"	H	1st Mich. S. S.	:	Right side, penetrated posterior of lung, lodging left side; ball extracted.
May 31, 1864.					
Putman, Orion........	Sergt.	C	2d "	:	Left foot, ball passed between first and second metacarpal.
Weston, James........	Pr.	D	" "	:	Right thigh, flesh; ball extracted.
Moppen, Henry........	Cor.	"	5th "	:	Abdomen, mortal; died June 1, 1864.
June 1, 1864.					
Farling, Amos........	Pr.	C	"	:	Left hand, flesh.
Welsh, John..........	"	B	"	:	Left foot, second and third toes.
Uxie, John S.........	"	C	"	:	Left thigh, flesh, lower third.
Mapes, Peter.........	"	D	"	:	Left humerus and elbow joint; amputated middle third.
Bennett, C. W........	"	C	"	:	Left leg, calf, flesh.
White, George........	"	H	"	:	Head, skull fractured; died June 2, 1864.
Perry, Abra..........	Sergt.	E	"	:	Left forearm, fracture, resection; three inches of radius, upper; extracted.

NORTH ANNA.—Continued.

Name.	Rank.	Co.	Regiment.	Missile.	Nature of Wound.
June 1, 1864.					
Leash, Hugh	Pr.	H	8th Mich.	Ball.	Right thigh; flesh.
Bracket, L. C.	1st Lieut.				Aid General Wilcox's staff. Left knee, contusion.
June 2, 1864.					
Row, Horace	Pr.	B	20th Mich.	Ball.	Neck, entered left side, exit between shoulders.
Essleman, F. J.	"	H	"	"	Left breast and arm.
Monroe, Gil.	"	"	"	"	Right arm.
Allbright, Frk.	"	B	"	"	Humerus, fracture, resection, large portion (not head), four inches.
Barney, Albt.	Sgt. Maj.		"	"	Left leg.
Clay, John	Pr.	E	"	"	Right breast, contusion.
Ikanbark, Nic.	"	H	"	"	Right instep, severe.
Scripture, Langdon	"	B	"	"	Right thigh, flesh.
Burlingame, Ron.	Cor.	A	"	"	Left forearm, resection, middle third of ulna.
Walker, Hiram.	Pr,	"	"	"	Left forearm, flesh.
McDole, Wm.	"	F	"	"	Back, ball remaining.

The lay of the ground at North Anna did not seem to please the general-in-chief, and he resolved to seek some point on the line towards Richmond, where Lee could not hold the interior line.

Up to this date the Army of the Potomac had been compelled, as we swung by our left flank, to travel three miles to the rebels' one. So, on the night of the 2d, we retraced our steps across the North Anna and swung around into position near Bethesda Church, a point secured by Sheridan the night before.

Just before day on the morning of the 3d both armies stood face to face as they had previously at the Wilderness, Spottsylvania, Nye River and North Anna. The whole army had never been asked by Grant or Meade to make a general charge previous to this, but flank movements to gain position had been the order of the day, and from this the army had been led to suppose, it would seem, that no other duty would be required of them. But Grant was a determined, though silent, man, and I believe there are but few living today who really understood him. It seems to me as though he wished to teach his army this great lesson, viz., that although he required great sacrifices of them, they must be *ever* ready and willing to make them.

June 3, 1864, is a day that will long be remembered both by the North and the South.

Each army was confident of victory, and just as the sun's rays began to dispel the darkness of those Virginia pines, the word was given for a general advance, which was obeyed with alacrity by every man, they being only too eager for the fight. But, as found at North Anna, Lee's army held the interior line. Two of his men were equal to five of ours. He had but about a mile of his line to defend, whereas we had three of ours, and it is not surprising to my readers that the main army was quickly repulsed.

We left nearly two thousand dead men on that bloody field, conveying all we possibly could of the ten thousand five hundred and seventy wounded to White-house Landing, the former home of Martha Washington, where, when a widow, she was courted and afterward married by her illustrious husband. Depot hospitals were established here on the York river, giving us a good point from which to ship our wounded North.

About two or three o'clock in the afternoon

of the 3d, General Grant ordered Meade to make a general advance and storm the rebel works again, which the whole army refused to do. So, the next evening, the 4th, by a left half wheel, we crossed the Chickahominy without any particular annoyance from the enemy, and reached Wilcox Landing, on James river, on the morning of the 16th of June, 1864.

The names of the wounded brought to field hospital at Cold Harbor June 3, 1864, are as follows:

BATTLE OF COLD HARBOR.

Name.	Rank.	Co.	Regiment.	Missile.	Nature of Wound.
Bachelder, Chas.	Pr.	B	8th Mich.	Ball.	Right femur.
Moody, Samuel	Maj	"	27th "	"	Right wrist, fractured; amputated at lower third.
Garland, Lewis	Pr.	I	" "	"	Left hand.
Watson, Andrew	"	B	" "	"	Neck and right shoulder.
Putman, James	Cor.	F	" "	"	Right shoulder.
Davis, James	Pr.	2 S. S.	" "	"	Left cheek, lodged in opposite maxillary.
O'Brien, Michael	"	A	" "	"	Back.
Vanluraneburg, G.	"	K	2d "	Grape.	Left humerus, fractured; amputated upper third.
Milton, Benjamin	Sergt.	F	" "	Ball.	Right breast, entered near clavicle, exit at right shoulder.
Hall, Gilbert	Pr.	I	27th "	"	Left shoulder, scapula fractured.
Wood, Washington	Cor.	C	8th "	"	Right calf.
Mickle, Wellington	Pr.	K	27th "	"	Right wrist.
Waldon, Welcome	"	C	8th "	"	Right chest, penetrating.
Miller, James	"	H	" "	"	Right side, floating ribs; ball removed.
Cooper, Henry	"	D	27th "	"	Right side, floating ribs; ball removed.
Miner, Douns	"	I	" "	"	Chin, slight flesh wound.
Ploof, Julius	"	E	8th "	"	Left humerus, fractured; resection of upper third.
Thompson, John	"	I	27th "	"	Right side, slight.

THE GREAT REBELLION.

Name	Rank	Co.	Reg.		Wound
Heath, Andrew	"	C	"	"	Right arm and shoulder; ball extracted.
Dryer, Henry	"	H	8th	"	Frontal bone fractured; exudation of brain matter.
Lewis, W. E.	Maj		"	"	Abdomen, mortal; died June 3d, 1864.
Giles, W. C.	Pr.	B	"	"	Left thigh, flesh.
Wolf, C.	"	I	"	"	Left cheek.
McCormick, J.	"	C	1st Mich. S. S	"	Left side and back.
Stoner, A. W.	"	B	8th	"	Right foot, great toe.
Weaver, H.	"	K	"	"	Left arm.
Hunt, Harmon	"	H	"	"	Right hand, fore finger.
Goodwell, And.	"	C	"	"	Left arm.
Childs, Phil.	"	B	"	Buckshot	Right arm, entered two inches above elbow; exit near wrist, nine inches from point of entry.
Mosher, H.	Capt.	G	"	Ball.	Left leg.
Belcher, Hora.	Pr.	"	"	"	Right elbow.
Phillips, Geo.	"	K	"	"	Right arm, penetrating chest.
Dennis, Everret	"	E	"	"	Right leg, slight, contusion.
Beardsley, Chas.	"	"	"	"	Right foot, ball of great toe.
Burnham, F.	"	C	"	"	Right side, contused.
Holmes, Wm.	"	F	"	"	Left leg.
Shank, Dan.	Cor.	"	"	"	Left thigh, ball remains.
McKinzie, Dan.	Pr.	K	"	"	Right foot.
Hersher, Chas.	"		"	"	Right cheek and mouth, fractured, injuring maxillary.

BATTLE OF COLD HARBOR.—Continued.

Name.	Rank.	Co.	Regiment.	Missile.	Nature of Wound.
Garish, Joe	Pr.	F	8th Mich.	Ball.	Left knee joint, severe; amputated lower third.
Doty, Daniel	"	B	"	"	Left side, between floating ribs, exit at hips.
Spencer, Harvey	"	F	"	"	Right, fractured, left humerus, penetrating abdomen.
Croy, Jacob	"	E	"	"	Entered above left iliac, ball remains.
Cash, Daniel	Adj.		27th		Abdomen, contusion, slight.
Vandevear, Wm	Pr.	2 S. z.	"	Shell.	Neck and between shoulders, slight contusion.
McCaltz, James	"	F	"	Ball.	Right thigh, flesh.
Marsh, Ed	"	H	8th	"	Right ankle, amputated lower third.
Dingham, Celon	"	F	27th	"	Left thigh nearly off; amputated upper third; died June 3, 1864.
Van Camp, J.	"	E	"	"	Left thigh, flesh.
Hines, Willis	"	G	"	"	Foot, great toe joint.
Remington, Ed	Sergt.	B	"	"	Left leg, flesh.
Case, Geo	Pr.	G	"	"	Left leg, third metacarpal.
Schloff, Henry	Cor.	B	"	"	Left side, contusion.
Wheeler, Ed	"	G	"	"	Chest.
Bremen, J. W.	1st Lieut.	"	"	"	Left breast, contusion.
Mar, Joseph	Pr.	F	"	"	Left breast and chest, passing through abdomen, exit floating ribs; died June 3, 1864.
Hicks, Wm	"	"	"	"	Abdomen, severe.

THE GREAT REBELLION.

Name	Rank	Co.			Cause	Wound
Mitchell, Antony	Sergt.	F	"			Left thigh.
Bropley, John	1st Lieut.	H	"			Both legs, flesh.
Trash, John	Pr.	I	"			Breast, contusion.
Miller, Charles	2d Lieut.	C	"			Chest, penetrating.
Vanhorn, John	Pr.	E	"			Left great toe and metatarsus.
Pearsall, R.	"	C	"			Abdomen.
Miller, Geo.	"	1 S. S.	"			Right foot, great toe.
Dansmore, Joe	"	"	"			Left foot, great toe joint.
Lalourette, John	"	"	"			Left forearm, contusion.
Hemminger, Levi	"	B	"			Leg, at ankle.
Cramer, Silas	"	G	"			Right hand, forefinger.
Carey, John	"	D	"			Right foot, fractured, ankle joint; amputated lower third of leg.
Spencer, Tho.	"	2 S. S.	"			Right hand thumb.
Blackmer, E.	"	"	"		Shell.	Hip, flesh.
Henney, Hiram	"	D	"		Ba.l.	Left forearm, contusion.
Dillen, Tho.	"	G	"			Right hip, flesh.
Southwart, Silas	Cor.	I	"			Right heel, flesh.
Rock, Peter	Pr.	C	"		Shell.	Right ankle, fractured; amputated ankle joint.
Dennison, Jabez	"	I	"		Ball.	Left hip, slight.
Wernsley, C.	"	F	"			Right shoulder, entered scapula; ball not found.
Wells, Sam	"	2 S. S.	"			Right shoulder, severe; amputated; exit upper third.

BATTLE OF COLD HARBOR.—Continued.

Name.	Rank.	Co.	Regiment.	Missile.	Nature of Wound.
Belden, W.	Pr.	K	27th Mich.	Shell.	Neck, slight.
Doty, Franklin	"	A	"	"	Right shoulder, penetrating chest, mortal; died June 3, 1864.
Fairfield, J.	"	B	"	"	Head, contusion, over right eye.
Kauf, J.	Sergt.	A	"	"	Right hand, thumb.
Grey, Clarke	Pr.	I	"	"	Right shoulder, penetrating abdomen; died June 3, 1864.
Armstrong, Geo.	"	A	"	Shell.	Laceration of forehead.
Connant, W.	"	K	"	Ball.	Right thumb.
Lombart, Wm.	"	H	"	"	Left hand, severe.
Hurd, Alb.	"	"	"	"	Left thigh, slight.
Hason, Emery	"	"	20th "	"	Right thigh, flesh.
Livingstone, H.	"	"	"	"	Head, left, scalp.
Muscott, Tho.	Cor.	"	"	"	Left thigh, severe.
Minnie, Gregory	Pr.	"	"	"	Left hand, thumb and second finger.
Bohner, Adam	"	"	"	"	Right thigh, flesh.
Odsen, Geo.	"	"	"	"	Right thigh, flesh.
Hand, Enoch	"	"	"	"	Head, scalp wound, behind left ear.
Link, Michael	"	"	"	"	Left breast, contusion.
Cullen, Pat.	"	"	"	"	Abdomen, severe.

THE GREAT REBELLION.

Name	Rank	Co.	Regt.		Wound
Dunn, Levi	Cor.	"	"	"	Forehead, scalp.
Sma, Ralph	Colorbear.	"	"	"	Left hip, laceration.
Suttard, Wm	Pr.	"	"	"	Right foot, contusion.
Everly, Mich	"	"	"	"	Left thigh, flesh, over left ear.
Whitmore, Fontille	"	"	4th "	"	Head, scalp wound.
Wayanberment, M	"	"	1st Mich. S. S.	"	Back, contusion.
Also, Chas	"	"	27th "	"	Left hip, exit right hip.
Morton, Ira	"	"	"	"	Left hip.
Train, R. E.	"	C	27th "	"	Ankle, contusion.
Kelley, Nelson	"	G	"	"	Chest, entered left floating ribs, exit left side; died June 3, 1864.
Wyllard, M	Cor.	K	"	"	Hand, first and second fingers.
Evens, Rbt.	Pr.	E	"	"	Right shoulder.
Spencer, S	"	2 S. S.	"	"	Chest, penetrated from side to side; died June 4, 1864.
Percival, Wm	"	F	"	"	Left eyelid, very slight.
Skinner, C.	Sergt.	H	"	"	Left shoulder, ball remains.
Williams, G	1st Lieut.	E.	2d "	"	Left hip, ball not found.
Feshal, G	Pr.	E	"	"	Left foot, fourth metatarsal.
Petgold, H	Cor.	H	"	"	Right hip.
Rassls, Jo	Pr.	C	"	"	Right arm, flesh wound, just above shoulder.
Stannard, Her	Sergt.	F	"	"	Right forearm.
Baker, Isaac	"	K	"	"	Left arm and forearm.

BATTLE OF COLD HARBOR.—*Continued.*

Name.	Rank.	Co.	Regiment.	Missile.	Nature of Wound.
McElvain, C.	Pr.	D	2d Mich.	Ball.	Thigh, flesh, severe.
Wingert, Caleb	"	G	8th "	"	Left leg, fibula and tibia, fractured; amputated.
Cook, Owen	Cor.	D	" "	"	Left shoulder, penetrating left lung; died June 3' 1864.
Hughes, G. W.	Pr.	B	" "	"	Left hand, fourth and fifth metacarpal.
Collier, W.	Sergt.	H	" "	"	Left hand, third and fourth metacarpal; removed.
Brow, James	Pr.	B	" "	"	Right hand, first and second fingers, index finger amputated.
Graham, J.	"	2 S. S.	27th "	"	Left hip.
Lewis, John	"	"	" "	"	Left lung penetrated.
Andrews, Tru.	"	C	20th "	"	Right leg fractured, and right shoulder.
Obsien, Tim	"	B	2d "	"	Head, scalp wound.
Albert, Frank	Sergt.	F	20th "	"	Right arm, just above elbow joint.
Carpenter, H.	2d Lieut.	A	" "	"	Right cheek, flesh.
Hu'er, Mar.	Pr.	K	" "	"	Right hand, severe; amputated.
Darling, Joe	"	G	" "	"	Right leg and elbow joint.
Socks, Peter	"	H	" "	"	Left thigh.
Zimmerman, George	Cor.	F	" "	Shell.	Right leg, near ankle.
Campbell, M.	Pr.	D	" "	"	Left thigh.
Copeland, W.	"	A	8th "	"	Head, scalp.

THE GREAT REBELLION.

Name	Rank	Co.	Regt.		Type	Wound
Joslin, Holden	"	K	"	"	"	Back, contusion between shoulders.
Spencer, Lucius	"	B	1st Mich. S.S.		Ball.	Left side, penetrating chest, mortal; died June 3, 1864.
Keller, Geo	Sergt.	I	2d "		"	Left ankle, contusion.
Skinner, B. H	Cor.	G	20th "		"	Left hand, fifth metacarpal.
Bidwell, D	Sergt.	C	" "		"	Right femur fracture.
Barka, R	Pr.	K	2d "		"	Left side, penetrating cavity of abdomen; died June 3, 1864.
Hank, Alvin	"	D	" "		"	Right hand, thumb shot off; accidental.
Willison, Sam	"	C	" "		Sld shot.	Right foot, contusion, severe.
Wolby, James	"	H	27th "		Shell.	Left wrist and breast, severe.
Manser, Jacob	Cor.	G	20th "		Ball.	Head, entered at right cheek, lodged right side of throat.
French, Geo	"	A	27th "		"	Tibula.
June 4, 1864.						
Morse, Oliver	Pr.	B	8th "		"	Right hand, index and second finger.
Ward, Geo	Cor.	"	20th "		"	Right testicle, contusion.
Brokaw, James	Pr.	F	" "		"	Right wrist, contusion.
June 5, 1864.						
Hart, And	"	D	1st Mich. S.S.		"	Right leg, severe.
Snook, Adam	"	"	8th "		"	Right groin.
Dermott, John	"	C	20th "		Shell.	Chest, contusion by limb of tree building earthworks.
June 6, 1864.						
Broker, John	"	F	2d "		Ball.	Both thighs, flesh.

BATTLE OF COLD HARBOR.—Continued.

Name.	Rank.	Co.	Regiment.	Missile.	Nature of Wound.
June 7, 1864.					
Alland, R.	Sergt.	I	20th Mich.	Ball.	Right side, flesh.
June 8, 1864.					
Marshal, W.	Col's. cook	H	2d "	Sld shot.	Right foot, severe.
Glover, Alden	Pr.	E	27th "	Ball.	Axilla, severe.
Voorhes, Jackson	"	I	" "	"	Left temple, grazed.
McHughes, Jas.	"	M	" "	"	Right breast, passing down to cavity of abdomen; died June 8, 1864.
Coats, Brazilla	"	K	2d "	"	Foot, small toe; amputated.
Green, Wm.	"	K	1st Mich. S. S.	"	Left arm and forearm and chest, penetrating; died June 8, 1864.
June 9, 1864.					
Hunt, Peter	Pr.	I	2d "	"	Right hand, ring finger; amputated.
Jones, Walter	"	B	" "	"	Left arm and left side.
June 10, 1864.					
Dickenson, M.	Muscn.	F	8th "	"	Left leg, calf, flesh.
Hoovey, Hedger	Pr.	G	1st "	"	Left hand, little finger.
June 11, 1864.					
Munger, Seth	Pr.	K	8th "	"	Right hand, third metacarpal
Knight, Cerene	2d Lieut.	D	1st Mich. S. S.	"	Right leg, calf, flesh.

June 13, 1864.				
Davis, George	Sergt.	G	1st "	Left hand, severe.
June 16, 1864.				
Ford, Jas. P.	Pr.	G	27th "	Right hand and index and second fingers.
Stephen, Geo.	"	H	8th "	Right thigh.
Willetts, Isaac	"	D	1st Mich. S. S.	Left foot, second toe; amputated.
Vellot, Wilson	"	"	27th "	Right foot, toe; amputated; supposed intentionally.

CHAPTER V.

It had been clearly understood that it was General Grant's intention, should he not succeed in defeating Lee before we reached Richmond, he would place the army south of the James river. He had, therefore, ordered Butler to move his troops to a convenient point on that side of the river to cover our crossing, should the necessity arise.

Sheridan's raid (the battle of Yellow Tavern) had apprised him of what was expected of him, and "old Ben" was right on hand, and the whole Army of the Potomac crossed, without any material accident, on the evening of the 15th and morning of the 16th of June, 1864.

We had about fifty of our division wounded by the withdrawal from the front, and not having time to communicate with our depot at White-house Landing again, we were compelled to take them with us to the James. The steamer "Mary Martin" was lying there, and every convenience which could contribute to the comfort of the wounded and relief of the hospital corps was readily supplied. The whole of the medical staff, from the excessive labor they had undergone, were nearly worn out transporting the wounded to safe quarters, but now came a relaxation that was welcome to all.

The hospital train of our division, as previously stated, crossed the James at Willcox Landing, our pontoons being laid the day previous. After we were well over on the south side our surgeon-in-chief said, "Boys, let us have a rest." Surgeon Bonine of the 2d, who outranked all the surgeons of the division, carried, with other good qualities, a tender heart. Kindness always beamed from his dear old eyes. But I do not intend to laud this action of his, for I think he was equally as anxious as the boys for a rest. It was certainly a lovely day, and we were only too willing to lay down and take a big sleep without much persuasion. I remember we were all stretched out on the grass, enjoying ourselves, about seven o'clock, our ambulances being all empty and no wounded to care for. Oh, what a luxurious sleep that was, to be sure, but when we awoke it was to hear the news that we were to move rapidly to the front of Petersburg, where we arrived and established headquarters about a mile and a half south of that historic little village in Central Virginia.

Grant had ordered General Butler to seize Petersburg the day before, which he did not accomplish.

Hancock did not understand what was expected of him, and I presume it was the same with Warren and Burnside, as it was not customary, except upon very important occasions, for Grant to inform one of his corps commanders what he expected of the other. Be that as it may, we found a heavy battle raging on our arrival, and in a short time the wounded commenced to arrive. But as night fell there was a cessation of hostilities until the morning of the 17th, when commencing again it continued all that day and the next until the 18th of June.

The following is a list of the wounded in the battles at and near Petersburg, June 17, 1864:

UNION GENERALS.

BATTLES AT AND NEAR PETERSBURG, JUNE 17, 1864.

Name.	Rank.	Co.	Regiment.	Missile.	Nature of Wound.
Rumphrey, F.	Pr.	D	1st Mich. S. S.	Ball.	Left elbow, flesh.
Nealons, J.	"	B	20th "	"	Right hand, second metacarpal.
Campbell, T.	1st Lieut	A	8th "	"	Head, entered over left eye, penetrating brain, exit crown of head; died June 17, 1864.
Smith, Berry	Pr.	H	1st Mich. S. S.	"	Right hand and wrist, joint.
Britt, C.	"	"	2d "	Shell.	Head, left side.
Glynn, T.	"	I	" "	Ball.	Head, left side.
Sessions, J.	Sergt.	"	" "	Grape.	Left arm near shoulder, resection of head of humerus and two inches of shaft; grape, exit front breast.
Huntoon, Isaac	Pr.	D	27th "	Ball.	Right hip.
Myers, Chas.	"	"	" "	"	Left cheek, near eye.
Kreps, Wm.	"	K	2d "	"	Right leg.
Gozenger, J.	"	I	20th "	"	Left hip.
Stafford, M.	Cor.	E	2d "	Shell.	Right leg shot away; died June 18, 1864.
Horrigan, Michael	Pr.	I	1st Mich. S. S.	Ball.	Head and left shoulder; ball extracted.
McKinsey, Wm.	"	B	27th Mich.	"	Left foot, instep.
Dunn, J.	Sergt.	G	2d "	Grape.	Left forearm.
Feetes, Ed.	Pr.	"	" "	Ball.	Right hip.
Menadue, J.	Sergt.	A	27th "	"	Head, scalp wound.

BATTLES AT AND NEAR PETERSBURG.—*Continued.*

Name.	Rank.	Co.	Regiment.	Missile.	Nature of Wound.
Groff, Joe	Sergt.	A	27th Mich.	Ball.	Right foot.
Truckey, Nelson	Capt.	B	"	"	Right leg, near ankle joint.
McIntyre, H.	Pr.	K	20th "	"	Right arm, near shoulder joint.
Scharf, Fred.	"	B	27th "	"	Right arm.
Pinney, Judson	"	K	8th "	Shell.	Left hip, contusion.
Ford, Herman	"	1 S. S.	27th "	"	Left shoulder.
Messil, J.	"	K	8th "	"	Left forearm.
Coy, Stephen	"	"	2d "	"	Left foot, severe, lower third leg, amputated.
Chapman, O.	"	E	" "	"	Left arm, flesh.
South, Hart.	Cor.	F	27th "	"	Head, severe.
Pearce, Wm.	Pr.	2 S. S.	" "	"	Back, contusion.
Davis, L.	"	H	" "	"	Left leg, ball extracted.
Smith, C.	"	D	2d "	"	Left shoulder and back.
Austin, R.	"	A	27th "	"	Left thigh.
Hinds, Chas.	"	G	2d "	Ball.	Abdomen; mortal.
Green, Myron	"	B	" "	"	Right leg fractured; amputated leg.
Tompkins, Joe	"	F	" "	"	Left shoulder.
Wood, James	Cor.	A	" "	"	Left shoulder.

THE GREAT REBELLION.   107

Name	Rank	Co.	Regiment	Cause	Injury
Vandebogart, W	"	F	"	"	Both thighs.
Miltenkamp, H	Pr.	B	20th "	Shell.	Right elbow.
Ganst, P	Cor.	"	2d "	"	Right eye-lid, right third finger.
Freeman, Dan	Pr.	"	"	Ball.	Right, first and second fingers.
Vrooman, H	"	"	"	Shell.	Right knee, contusion.
Gardner, Nels	"	"	"	"	Left humerus, fracture.
Stewart, Wm	"	"	"	"	Right leg, just below knee.
Woolsey, Geo	"	"	20th "	Ball.	Left leg, below knee.
Kimball, Abe	"	"	2d "	Shell.	Left ankle, contusion.
Hatch, Luke	"	"	1st Mich. S. S.	Ball.	Left forearm.
Tracey, John	"	"	2d "	Shell.	Right ribs, contusion.
Kedle, John	"	"	1st Mich. S. S.	"	Fracture of skull.
White, John	Pr.	H	2d Mich	Ball.	Right thigh.
Gaygutch, Sam	"	K	1st Mich. S. S.	"	Right forearm.
Chatfield, Cha	"	K	"	"	Back, contusion.
Hays, Geo	Cor.	K	2d "	"	Left knee, severe, and right.
Stewart, Fk	"	B	1st Mich. S. S.	"	Left thigh.
Fairchild, S	"	F	20th "	"	Back of neck and spine; paralysis, lower parts of body.
Collins, Char	"	B	1st Mich. S. 9.	"	Right thigh.
McCray, James	"	H	2d "	Canist'r.	Left hip.
Voss, John	Sergt.	K	"	Ball.	Left ankle.

BATTLES AT AND NEAR PETERSBURG.—Continued.

Name.	Rank.	Co.	Regiment.	Missile.	Nature of Wound.
Gaffeny, Tho.	Capt.	G	1st Mich. S. S.	Ball.	Left shoulder.
Fry, John.	Pr.	K	" "	Shell.	Contusion, right gluteal.
Slate, Willard.	Sergt.	A	" "	"	Right arm above elbow.
Graveast, G.	2d Lieut.	K	" "	"	Left forearm, fracture.
Brown, E.	Sergt.	C	" "	Ball.	Right thigh.
Pierce, Silas.	Pr.	B	" "	"	Neck, left side.
Dean, Wm.	"	D	" "	"	Left ankle, flesh.
Fazier, J.	"	C	" "	"	Left leg and thigh, fracture.
Levenson, Knud	"	B	2d "	"	Left wrist, fracture; amputated above wrist.
Fish, J.	"	F	" "	"	Left elbow, fracture.
Murdock, G.	Capt.	I	" "	"	Right side, head.
Hall, Eugene	Pr.	O	1st Mich. S. S.	"	Right hip.
Diamond, J.	"	F	8th "	"	Skull fractured; died during night, June 20, 1864.
Munson, John	"	E	2d "	"	Left calf, flesh.
Fellinger, M.	"	H	1st Mich. S. S.	Shell.	Contusion of lumbar vertebræ; died June 18, 1864.
Derthick, A.	Cor.	F	2d "	Ball.	Left third toe.
Meter, Ernest.	Pr.	G	27th "	"	Right thigh, fracture.
Helm, Manasus.	"	B	20th "	"	Left shoulder, contusion.

Name	Rank	Co.	Regiment		Weapon	Wound
Curtis, Ralph	Cor.	C	2d	"	"	Right leg.
Sullivan, N.	Pr.	H	"	"	Shell.	Left lower leg, fractured.
Collins, Frank	"	E	"	"	Ball.	Left thigh, also rupture, right side.
McKeever, Neal	"	C	"	"	"	Very slight contusion.
Ellsworth, R. H.	"	"	27th	"	"	Right lower leg.
Hoffman, Amos	Cor.	"	1st Mich. S. S.	"	"	Left thigh.
McCuan, Geo.	Pr.	H	2d	"	"	Right ankle.
Stewart, Joe	Cor.	B	27th	"	"	Back, flesh.
Lieber, Ch.	Pr.	D	"	"	"	Second left toe.
Moxey, Henry	"	H	2d	"	"	Left hand.
Merrils, Hiram	Muscn.	B	8th	"	Shell.	Left thigh.
Atwood, James	Pr.	K	"	"	Ball.	Contusion, right ankle.
Jennie, Asa	"	G	2d	"	"	Secrets and left knee.
Schuyler, Casper	Cor.	C	27th	"	"	Chest; died June 17, 1884.
Ould, Andrew	Pr.	D	2d	"	"	Left hand.
Freeland, A.	"	B	"	"	"	Right knee.
Smith, Geo.	Cor.	E	"	"	"	Left thumb and index finger.
Smith, Ch.	"	"	"	"	"	Left calf.
Smith, Dennis	"	K	"	"	Shell.	Contusion, right leg.
Isbell, L.	Pr.	F	27th	"	Ball.	Right hand.
Newman, F.	Cor.	A	8th	"	"	Left calf; dead.

BATTLES AT AND NEAR PETERSBURG.—*Continued.*

Name.	Rank.	Co.	Regiment.	Missile.	Nature of Wound.
Ford, Val	Pr.	K	8th Mich.	Ball.	Left breast.
Lane, Rob	"	A	27th "	"	Left side, lodged in right.
Sellman, R.	"	B	" "	"	Right calf.
Conn, C. G.	2d Lieut.	G	1st Mich. S. S.	"	Left forearm, flesh.
Ralph, H. S.	Pr.	E	" "	"	Left lower leg, flesh.
Reely, Geo.	"	C	27th "	"	Left forearm and upper arm and contusion.
Hartman, O.	"	B	2d "	"	Back, near right lower angle of scapula.
Rudabough, T.	"	D	" "	"	Left upper arm.
Mullen, W.	"	A	" "	"	Right hand.
Newton, Aug.	"	F	8th "	"	Left thigh.
Stearns, Ed.	"	"	20th "	"	Right shoulder.
Bowers, Lew	"	"	" "	"	Left hand.
Whiting, Ed.	"	"	8th "	"	Contusion, right hand.
Hall, H.	"	K	2d "	"	Left thigh.
Rodgers, Wm.	"	C	" "	"	Right lower leg.
Jones, Nicholas	"	I	27th "	"	Left wrist.
Newton, Ch.	Cor.	A	" "	"	Right thigh.
Snook, Ch.	Pr.	E	2d "	"	Chest.

THE GREAT REBELLION. 111

Name	Rank	Co.			Type	Wound
Wheeler, Ernest	"	"	"	"	Grape.	Contusion, left foot.
Rutty, Henry	"	F	27th	"	"	Contusion, left ankle.
Johnson, Sid	"	C	2d	"	"	Left foot, between great and second toe.
Roll, Anthony	"	E	"	"	"	Left lower leg.
Rogers, Sand	"	A	"	"	"	Right thigh.
Leonard, Sm	"	I	"	"	"	Right thigh.
Osgood, Ch	"	F	27th	"	"	Left side.
Carter, Mich	"	E	2d	"	"	Right hip.
Edinger, E. W.	Cor.	"	"	"	"	Left hip.
Howell, James	Pr.	B	27th	"	"	Right thigh.
Parker, Wm	"	G	2d	"	Ball.	Left foot.
Landers, V	"	D	8th	"	"	Right index finger.
Powitt, Nelson	"	B	2d	"	"	Both thighs.
Marlew, John	"	"	27th	"	"	Left arm.
Mangin, J. G.	Sergt.	"	"	"	"	Left leg.
Harper, Edwin	Pr.	G	"	"	"	Right side and neck.
Goover, Hira	Cor.	I	"	"	"	Both thighs; ball removed.
Mead, F. H.	1st Lieut.	C	"	"	"	Left ear, slight.
Mead, Ira	Pr.	H	2d	"	"	Right foot, ball extracted.
Marchefke, F.	"	E	"	"	"	Right leg.
Stone, Wesley	Sergt.	D	"	"	"	Left arm.

BATTLES AT AND NEAR PETERSBURG.—Continued.

Name.	Rank.	Co.	Regiment.	Missile.	Nature of Wound.
Bristol, Phil.	Pr.	D	8th Mich.	Ball.	Right hip.
Ewing, H.	"	D	" "	"	Above left eye.
Christ, G.	"	G	" "	"	Left leg.
Walsh, J.	"	G	1st Mich. S. S.	"	Right leg, fracture, skull.
Bettor, Rob.	"	B	2d "	"	Right leg, flesh.
Vallan, James	"	I	" "	"	Face, slight; ball extracted below and inside knee.
Stone, Antony	"	E	" "	Shell.	Left leg.
Hewett, John	"	A	8th "	Ball.	Right shoulder.
Roe, Frank	"	K	2d "	"	Skull, fracture.
Barner, Mat.	"	A	" "	"	Right arm and face.
Smith, Wm.	"	F	" "	"	Right side of nose.
Hanker, John	"	H	1st Mich. S. S.	"	Right shoulder.
Dutton, Luther	"	K	" "	"	Right thigh, flesh.
Thayer, Frk.	"	H	2d "	"	Left forearm.
Pontery, Peter	"	E	8th "	"	Left arm, slight.
Moore, Mat.	"	K	2d "	"	Frontal sinus, over left eye.
June 18, 1864.					
Hadden, Sand.	"	E		"	Left chin, slight.

THE GREAT REBELLION.

Name	Rank	Co.	Regt.		Cause	Wound
Fox, D. M.	Col.				"	Right arm.
Conrad, Clark	Pt.	I	27th		"	Left third finger.
O'Brien, Lyster	1st Lieut.	D	2d		Shell.	Right arm, contusion.
Thomas, Phil.	Pt.	I	27th		Ball.	Contusion, left elbow.
Payne, Dwight	"	F	27th		"	Index and second right fingers.
Barnes, Geo.	Maj.		27th		"	Entered left of right nipple; dead.
Pixley, Henry	Cor.	B	20th		"	Right metacarpal.
Adams, E. M.	2d Lieut.	F	2d		"	Scalp, severe.
Sherman, E.	1st Lieut.	D	20th		Shell.	Right hand, severe.
Jackson, Char.	Cor.	G	2d		"	Right wrist.
Bryan, Edgar	"	I	"		"	Third right finger.
Soule, Elijah	Pr.	E	20th		"	Right upper arm.
Harper, Ja.	"	A	1st		"	Right forearm.
Hungerford, W.	"	E	20th		"	Right upper arm.
Ranger, Nath.	"	H	2d		"	Left shoulder.
Wade, James	"	"	"		"	Right foot.
Maxwell, P.	"	F	20th		"	Right hand.
Hall, Eugene	Sergt.	D	"		"	Right lower leg.
Ehher, John	Pr.	F	2d		"	Flesh, head, slight.
Billings, A. C.	1st Sergt.	F	"		"	Right knee.
Robinson, W. H.	Pt.	"	"		Ball.	Right thigh, flesh.

BATTLES AT AND NEAR PETERSBURG.—Continued.

Name.	Rank.	Co.	Regiment.	Missile.	Nature of Wound.
Bennett, John W.	Pr.	E	20th Mich.	Ball.	Right thigh, flesh, slight.
Nover, Conrad	"	I	" "	"	Contusion, left thigh.
Knight, Andrew	Sergt.	C	" "	"	Right ankle.
Hath, Lyman	"	D	2d "	"	Right lower leg, fractured.
Sweet, Elias C.	Pr.	K	20th "	"	Right foot.
Riggs, Levi	"	H	" "	"	Entrance right temple, exit behind right ear.
Cook, George	2d Lieut.	B	2d "	"	Right foot.
Canby, David B.	Pr.	A	27th "	Grape.	Contusion, right knee.
Goodrich, Frank	Sergt.	K	2d "	Ball.	Fore and second finger, left hand.
Treadwell, Edson	Cor.	I	20th "	"	Right elbow.
Massey, George F.	Pr.	"	2d "	"	Forehead, flesh.
Langan, James	"	D	" "	"	Right knee joint; amputated thigh above condyles.
Templar, Nicolas	Cor.	A	20th "	"	Right side near intestines, exit near shoulder.
Gibson, William	Sergt.	C	27th "	"	Fracture, right tibia below knee; died June 18, 1864.
Perry, Thomas	Pr.	I	2d "	"	Left upper arm, flesh.
Smith, Henry W.	"	"	20th "	"	Left thumb, third and fourth fingers, left side contusion; thumb and finger (middle) left hand, amputated.
Schemerhorn, Frank	Cor.	E	" "	"	Entered under right arm, exit near spine.
Spicer, William	Pr.	G	" "	"	Between ankle joint and tendon achilles.

Name	Rank	Co.	Date		Wound
Jones, Ransom P.	"	F	"	"	Entered left side between eighth and ninth ribs.
Goulds, Charles	"	E	"	"	Right hand, fracture; fourth and fifth metacarpal bones, right hand.
Nibbling, John	"	B	"	"	Left side, face.
McCray, Joseph	"	G	2d	"	Privates and left thigh.
Boscow, Robert	"	C	"	"	Contusion, left shoulder.
Calhoun, Walter	Cor.	H	"	"	Left lower arm.
Havens, Daniel L.	Pr.	"	"	"	Right elbow joint.
Taylor, William	"	D	20th	"	Right wrist and both thighs.
Todd, M. C.	Sergt.	M	27th	"	Contusion, right thigh and testes.
Spitzler, Stephen	"	B	"	Grape.	Right nates.
Patterson, John	1st Lieut.	I	"	"	Contusion, both legs near ankle.
Lavan, Wm. O.	Cor.	B	20th	Ball.	Contusion lower end between right membrane, thumb split.
Sanders, Phillip	Pr.	I	"	"	Chest, ball penetrated below nipple, removed from right side of spine.
Hall, Lafayette	"	K	8th	"	Scalp, over left ear.
Ridney, Isaac J.	"	G	"	"	Scalp, slight.
Traut, Wilson	"	C	20th	"	Right tibia and fibula fractured near knee.
Weirs, Manuel	Cor.	M	27th	"	
Stevenson, Oliver J.	Pr.	C	20th	"	Flesh wound, right eye, slight.
Morley, William	"	D	2d	"	Right upper arm, flesh.
Brown, Isaac M.	"	C	20th	"	Right thigh above knee; ball remains.
Brown, Oscar A.	"	I	"	"	Contusion, left hip.

BATTLES AT AND NEAR PETERSBURG.—Continued.

Name.	Rank.	Co.	Regiment.	Missile.	Nature of Wound.
McKinsey, Daniel	Pr.	K	20th Mich.	Ball.	Left upper arm.
Carl, Janis E.	"	A	"	"	Fracture tibia, right side, flesh; right leg amputated at thigh.
Speckman, John	"	G	"	Shell.	Back, severe.
Boyce, Chas. M.	"	H	20th "	"	Contusion, chest.
Manton, Wm. H.	"	B	17th "	Ball.	Fracture, right tibia, ball through right tibia below knee.
Dillon, Thaddeus	"	H	20th "	Shell.	Contusion, abdomen, slight.
Wilson, William	"	M	27th "	"	Contusion, left groin.
Knecht, Frederick	"	D	2d "	Ball.	Entered left temple, exit under chin and contusion, breast.
Armstrong, Samuel	"	G	"	"	Fracture, left femur.
Sanford, Thos. H.	"	D	"	"	Right hand, flesh.
Henry, Merrill	"	G	27th "	Shell.	Right thigh, very severe; mortal; died June 19, 1864.
Craft, Ezra	"	G	"	Ball.	Second, third and fourth metacarpals, left hand.
Mulford, Nelson	"	G	2d "	"	Under right clavicle; penetrated chest; died June 19, 1864.
Robinson, C. L.	Sergt.	G	"	"	Right leg above knee, flesh wound.
Phillips, A. L.	Pr.	C	"	"	Left thigh and calf.
Miller, Wm. W.	"	C	"	"	Right foot and breast, slight.
Duesler, John R.	"	K	27th "	"	Left forefinger.
Woodruff, James H.	"	A	"	"	Left hand, slight.

Name	Rank	Co.	Regt.	Cause	Wound
Homill, James V.	"	F	2d	"	Left shoulder, severe; passing through spine, paralyzing limbs.
David, Philander	"	C	"	"	Left chest.
Mills, Rolla	"		1st Mich. S. S.	"	Right great toe.
Ormsby, Matthew	"	A	2d	"	Right floating ribs penetrating abdomen.
Irwin, Leamon	"	F	20th	"	Through from side to side above ilium through bowels transversely.
Place, Henry	"	K	27th	"	Left leg below knee, severe.
Hatch, George	"	D	2d	"	Fracture of skull, left temple, severe.
Fredericks, John	"	K	2d	"	Right lower leg fractured, severe.
Witt, James E.	"	H	"	"	Right breast, penetrating.
Bohner, Linary	"	M	27th	Shell.	Contusion, right breast.
Briggs, Oscar	"	H	20th	"	Contusion, right knee; amputated lower third femur.
Purchis, Christ.	"	G	27th	Ball.	Left index.
Tibbard, Jacob	Cor.	I	"	"	Left ankle, flesh.
Isbell, Henry	Pr.	"	"	"	Left shin, contusion.
Beecher, George	"	F	"	"	Chin, flesh.
Tricker, John	"	K	20th	"	Right ankle.
Henner, Henry	"	F	2d	"	Right foot, severe.
Copenhaven, Henry	"	H	27th	"	Left forearm, flesh.
Dingman, DeWitt	"	E	"	"	Left hand thumb and two fingers.
Picket, Chas.	"	"	20th	"	Upper arm, fracture, left resection four inches shaft of humerus.
Vosper, Richard	Capt.	M	27th	"	Contusion, left breast.

BATTLES AT AND NEAR PETERSBURG.—Continued.

Name.	Rank.	Co.	Regiment.	Missile.	Nature of Wound.
Whitman, William	Pr.	A	27th Mich.	Bal'.	Index and second fingers.
Shafer, William	"	E	20th "	"	Right shoulder, fractured.
Ramsey, J. W.	"	D	27th "	"	Contusion, left knee, slight.
King, Elias	"	S	" "	"	Right hip, severe; died June 18, 1864.
St. Andrew, Clen	"	B	" "	"	Left thigh fractured; died June 19, 1864.
Kine, Henry	Sergt.	A	8th "	"	Left humerus fractured.
Vangooda, John	Pr.	H	2d "	"	Left thumb and second finger.
Brant, William	"	M	27th "	"	Left upper arm, humerus.
Webster, Lewis	Sergt.	A	8th "	"	Over pubis, flesh.
Fitzgerald, Thos.	Pr.	"	27th "	"	Fourth metacarpal.
Meyer, Elias	"	"	" "	"	Left thigh, flesh.
Beaver, John	"	K	" "	"	Left forearm, flesh.
Gray, Chearkelson	"	I	8th "	"	Left wrist, fractured.
Cator, George	"	E	2d "	"	Left thigh, flesh.
Miller, Adam	"	A	8th "	"	Right humerus.
Vanchiviel, Walter	Cor.	E	" "	"	Right elbow.
Myron, Eden	Capt.	"	" "	"	Right calf.
Smith, David	Pr.	K	27th "	"	Left thigh, femur fractured.

THE GREAT REBELLION. 119

Name	Rank	Co.			Wound
Britton, J. S.	"	M	"		Right lumbar vertebra.
Whitman, George	"	A	"		Right side about seventh rib, penetrating chest.
Saxon, Fred	"	G	8th		Right shoulder, ball passing in front and to inner side of humerus, entered margin of scapula.
Hubbs, Chas.	"	E	"		Left thigh, flesh.
Owen, James E.	"	I	27th		Neck.
Outcalt, John W.	Cor.	"	"		Right lower-leg, flesh.
Coffin, John	Pr.	K	2d		Right thigh, flesh.
Sturgis, Hiram	"	F	8th		Left side, near scapula.
Mattoon, Geo. P.	"	I	27th		Scalp, back of right ear.
McCarthy, John	"	K	"		Middle left toe.
Alexander, Benton	"	D	2d		Left wrist, flesh.
Frield, George	"	G	27th		Sternum, penetrated chest and right thigh; died June 20, 1864.
Cole, Archibald	"	D	2d		Right breast, penetrated.
Caldwell, Roscoe	"	C	8th		Femur fractured, upper third.
Dunn, Richard	"	G	2d		Right shoulder.
Kelley, George L.	"	B	"		Left upper ———
Walton, Billy	"	C	8th		Left little finger.
Hammond, Elijah	"	B	2d		Left index and second finger.
Stettler, Shed H.	"	A	"		Back penetrated.
Wright Henry J.	"	C	"		Right femur fractured; amputated middle third.
Stewart, George	Cor.	H	27th		Right floating ribs, ball remains; died June 18, 1864.

BATTLES AT AND NEAR PETERSBURG.—Continued.

Name.	Rank.	Co.	Regiment.	Missile.	Nature of Wound.
Headley, James	Cor.	B	2d Mich.	Ball.	Right shoulder.
Handlin, James	Pr.	G	"	"	Left upper arm near elbow.
Hulee, Clere	Cor.	H	"	Grape.	Right thigh, fracture, femur; amputated left hip.
Croff, Nathan J.	Pr.	K	"	Ball.	Head and sole of left foot.
Keyes, George W.	"	E	"	"	Right knee joint.
McCollum, Lafayette	"	H	"	"	Right shoulder and arm, oblique fracture humerus, surgical neck extended four inches down shaft.
Lamain, William	"	"	27th "	"	Left tibia: amputation at middle third.
Hally, Chas.	"	"	2d "	"	Right thigh, fractured; amputated.
Bugby, Sullivan	"	"	27th "	"	Right breast.
Shehan, Wm.	"	B	"	"	Right thigh, flesh.
June 19, 1864.					
Wallace, John	"	G	1st Mich. S. S.	"	Through left foot.
March, E. J.	Lt. Col.		2d "	"	Back part of head, scalp.
Iasnoske, L.	Sergt.	E	27th "	"	Right forearm.
Lavush, Gust.	Pr.	B	"	"	Left forearm.
Megarah, John	Sergt.	F	"	"	Left thigh.
Johnson, Wm.	"	"	"	"	Right foot, severe.
Thegog, John	Pr.	K	1st Mich. S. S.	"	Right hand, flesh.

Name	Rank	Co.	Reg.		Wound
Young, Darwin	"	M	27th "	"	Left thigh, ball remains.
Dodge, Christ. L.	"	A	" "	"	Left breast, exit back under arm, flesh.
Barrett, Wm.	Cor.	F	8th "	"	Near right ankle, flesh, slight.
Snell, Albert	"	G	27th "	"	Contusion, left side.
June 20, 1864.					
Frentz, Albert	Pr.	2d	27th "	"	Left index finger, slight.
Shomin, John	"	K	1st Mich. S. S.	"	Left elbow.
Williams, Chas.	"	F	27th "	"	Fracture, forearm, by fall from horse.
Osterhouse, John	"	K	" "	"	Right knee, contusion.
Britton, Leroy	"	F	" "	"	Left thumb.
Wagger, Martin	2d Lieut.	F	1st Mich. S. S.	"	Fourth and fifth toes; returned to regiment.
Burton, Luther	Pr.	F	27th "	"	Entered left side nose, exit mouth.
June 21, 1864.					
Knowles, Geo. M.	Cor.	C	20th "	"	Right index finger, amputated first phalange; sent to regiment July 25, 1864. Entered left shoulder, passing under scapula, fracturing fifth rib; ball removed from lower angle scapula.
Allend, Wm. H.	Pr.	2 S. S.	27th "	"	
June 22, 1864.					
Parkhurst, D.	"	A	1st Mich. S. S.	"	Right thumb.
Whittock, Nelson	"	E	27th "	"	
Shipper, Albert	"	H	2d "	"	Right cheek, flesh.
Morehouse, Gilbert	"	C	1st Mich. S. S.	"	Right thigh, supposed fracture; upper third fractured, spicula removed.
Ramsey, James	"	I	" "	"	Right leg, flesh.

BATTLES AT AND NEAR PETERSBURG.—Continued.

Name.	Rank.	Co.	Regiment.	Missile.	Nature of Wound.
June 24, 1864.					
Brown, Kearney	Pr.	B	1st Mich. S. S.	Ball.	Right foot fractured, metacarpal bone, spicula removed; ball remains.
Sasserne, Narcissus	"	B	27th "	"	Right chest, slight.
Brandt, Chas.	"	D	8th "	"	Left foot.
June 23, 1864.					
Bergman, Fred.	"	E	27th "	"	Left hand, third finger amputated.
Carwin, Chas.	"	D	17th "	"	Left arm, upper.
June 24, 1864.					
Grey, Jedediah	"	C	1st Mich. S. S.	"	Small of back.
Bacheldor, A.	"	I	8th "	"	Chest and right arm.
Chero, William	"	K	2d "	"	Left thumb, slight.
Corkins, Milton	"	A	1st Mich. S. S.	"	Left hand, fracture of second metacarpal bone; amputated index finger.
Brow, James	"	E	20th "	"	Right thumb, tip of.
Durning, Thos.	"	F	1st Mich. S. S.	"	Left side.
Denton, Willis	Cor.	E	8th "	"	Entered three inches below outer side right nipple, exit raphle of scrotum superficial to pubis, thence wounding urethra.
Ewing, Andrew	"	D	2d "	"	Second finger, left hand, slight.
Gibbons, James	Pr.	B	" "	"	Right forearm.
Harper, Samuel	"	"	20th "	"	Entered above right mastoid bone, exit nose, course downward and inside; head wound; died June 25, 1864.
Jennings, A. B.	Cor.	A	8th "	"	Right thigh.

THE GREAT REBELLION. 123

June 25, 1864.					
Hodges, James H.	Pr.	G	2d	"	Entered in front of right armpit, exit above left nipple, fracturing sternum; died July 5, 1864.
Feaser, Henry	Sergt.	C	27th	"	Left elbow joint, internal condyle olecoanen fractured; amputated above elbow.
Null, Henry	Pr.	G	2d	"	Flesh wound, leg, popliteal space, slight; ball extracted.
Wager, Martin	Lieut.	F	1st Mich. S. S.		Head, penetrating mastoid process, temporal bones, left side, lodging in base of brain; died June 25, 1864.
Dibble, Clark	Pr.	G	8th "		Flesh wound, upper surface right shoulder.
Rickaby, R. W.	Capt.	A	2d Mich. S. S.		Left forearm, fracture, resection of two inches of lower third of radius; died July 2, 1864.
Jackson, Charles	Cor.	G	2d "		Left lower leg, partial resection upper third fibula, died July 2, 1864.
Allen, Derrick	Pr.	I	"	"	Ball entered neck.
June 26, 1864.					
Andrew, John	"	K	1st Mich. S. S.		Right thigh, near hip, flesh.
Huff, Asher	Cor.	I	" "	"	Flesh wound, left knee.
Doubleday, Smith	Pr.	G	8th "	"	Mortally wounded in head; died June 26, 1864.
Finen, Jerry	"	A	1st Mich. S. S.	"	Little toe, left foot; amputated.
Hoysington, Alonzo	"	"	8th "	"	Entered through center big patella, exit upper and inner edge of tibia, slightly denuding it.
June 27, 1864.					
Varnum, Joseph	Sergt.	A	2d	"	Entrance left glutei muscle opposite ilium, its line of exit at a point right side corresponding with entrance, making a third opening between the nates; flesh wound.
Heesen, Hendrick	Pr.	B	20th	"	Entering lobe of left ear, exit near outer canthus left eye, superficial; flesh wound.
Bingham, A. L.	Capt.	H	27th	"	Entrance dorsal, exit on palmer surface of right index finger metacarpel, joint wound.

BATTLES AT AND NEAR PETERSBURG.—Continued.

Name.	Rank.	Co.	Regiment.	Missile.	Nature of Wound.
June 27, 1864.					
McElroy, M.	Sergt.	C	27th Mich.	Ball.	Entrance near superior border of right scapula, passing under trapezia muscle, fracturing cervicle and upper dorsal vertebrae, fracturing spine, left scapula; ball extracted near head of left scapula.
Westbrook, Jonathan	Pr.	"	"	"	Entrance upper and middle occipital, exit left and inferior side of occipital.
Trus, George	"	E	8th "	"	Struck between thumb and ring finger, left hand, merely cutting web.
June 28, 1864.					
Sedelow, Joseph	Sergt.	G	27th "	"	Shattering second joint; right thumb amputated.
Arnold, Edwin	Pr.	F	2d "	"	Entered posterior to angle jaw, left side, exit below occipital protuberance; died June 29, 1864.
Bush, ▬▬▬in	"	E	17th "	"	Entered upper and posterior portion of temple bone, exit directly opposite; dead.
Burr, Turner	"	C	8th "	"	Entered left leg, inner side belly of gastronemia, exit directly opposite.
Smith, James	"	H	1st "	"	Entered above and posterior to trochanter, passed downward and inward; died July 2, 1864.
Hobenbeck, James	Cor.	I	8th "	"	Entrance near and exit right nipple, penetrating right lung, extracted between tenth and eleventh ribs of left side; died June 29, 1864.
Shultz, John E.	Pr.	A	2d "	"	Touching between third anterior and right side tibia, suppuration.
June 29, 1864.					
Steid, James Harrison	"	F	20th "	"	Entered central portion calf, left leg, exit opposite, near fibula, flesh.
McBain, Duncan	Sergt.	"	8th "	Shell.	Contusion of occiput and right shoulder, powder imbedded, not serious.
Sharp, Warner	"	"	1st "	Ball.	Left leg, entered inferior edge and touching right maleous, exit inferior and angular to left; died July 12, 1864.

THE GREAT REBELLION.

Name	Rank	Co.	Regt.	Description
Wally, Frederick	"	D	8th	Entered left leg between middle and upper third, anterior to bone, passing through right leg anterior to bone; died June 30, 1864.
June 30, 1864.				
Brown, Noble	"	B	2d	Entered palms surface left hand, exit opposite, fractured metacarpal of ring finger.
Crinfort, Thomas	"	H	27th	Left side, four inches posterior and in line with nipple, exit near side of scapula, rib fractured.
July 1, 1864.				
Priestly, Wm	"	D	2d	Entered back of and exit palmer surface of left hand, between metacarpals of ring and middle fingers.
Fitzpatrick, J.	"	A	27th	Face, grazed left cheek, passing upwards and forward, entering left ala of nose, extracted.
Pike, Murray S.	Cor.	2 S. S.	2d	Dorsal and near big toe, exit opposite left.
Peck, Edwin	Pr.	"	"	Left side head; died July 3, 1864.
July 2, 1864.				
Scott, Edward	Sergt.	K	8th	Entrance left side, two inches anterior to angle and between seventh and eighth ribs, lodging near spine.
Smith, Henry C	Cor.	E	"	Entrance outer condyle of left humerus, exit three inches below elbow joint; amputated above elbow.
Sinner, Theodore	Pr.	C	27th	Grazed toe and ball of left foot, slight.
Richard, Alexander	Sergt.	B	2d	Passed through left foot, accidental.
Wilber, Charles	Pr.	"	"	Shattered first phalange of middle finger, amputated.
July 3, 1864.				
Ford, Robert	"	H	"	Back, entered middle left scapula, exit near inferior right scapula; paralysis below point of injury; died July 5, 1864.
Root, James	"	D	"	Entered anterior and middle third left leg, grazing tibia, exit opposite; flesh.
King, George	"	"	"	Left, superficiary ridge, flesh.
Geller, Augustus	"	I	20th	Left scapula; flesh.

BATTLES AT AND NEAR PETERSBURG.—Continued.

Name.	Rank.	Co.	Regiment.	Missile.	Nature of Wound.
July 4, 1864.					
O'Connell, Patrick	Pr.	B	8th Mich.	Shell.	Contusion, finger and shoulder, left arm; slight.
Robinson, Alexander	"	"	"	"	Fractured left clavicle, contusion, muscles of arm, contusion of carpal and metacarpal, lower, of ring and middle finger, right arm; died July 5, 1864.
Kimball, David	"	D	27th "	Ball.	Shattered last phalange of index and middle fingers of right hand; amputated.
July 5, 1864.					
Berry, Joseph	Lieut.	A	2d "	"	Grazed left nates: sent to regiment July 25, 1864.
July 6, 1864.					
Miller, Charles	Pr.	"	"	"	Entrance inferior and near little toe, exit inferior of great toe; sent to general hospital July 10, 1864.
Brines, George	"	C	27th "	"	Grazed right breast, entered outer edge of tendon of pectoralis major muscles, exit anterior surface of right arm.
Hett, John P	"	E	"	"	Contusion, flesh below sternum; sent to general hospital July 10, 1864.
July 7, 1864.					
Johnson, R. D	Capt.	I	2d "	"	Left thigh near scrotum, ball passed upward and backward; extracted below entrance.
Parker, Wallace	Pr.	F	"	"	Left thigh, anterior side of nates, passing directly through; ball extracted opposite; sent to general hospital July 12, 1864.
Lane, George	"	2 S. S.	27th "	"	Spent, grazed anterior portion of scrotum and right groin, passing upward; sent to general hospital July 10, 1864.
Hall, Francis	"	K	17th "	"	Right thigh, entered upper and inner side, exit anterior and middle third.

THE GREAT REBELLION. 127

Name	Rank	Co.	Regt.	Weapon	Description
July 8, 1864.					
Perrine, Henry	"	F	2d	"	Left arm, entered near anterior condyle of humerus, exit inner and middle third, left arm; course upward and inward; sent to gen'l hospital July 10, '64.
More, Christian	"	K	8th	"	Head, left side, entered middle temporal bone, exit anterior border of sternum mastoid muscle.
Danlon, Michael	"	C	27th	Shell	Nose, entered at nasal bone, imbedded in nasal cavity; ball extracted through entrance, spicula removed.
Bradley, Robert	"	H	1st	Ball	Head contusion, left parietal eminence; sent to general hospital July 10, 1864.
Burgess, Thomas	"	C	27th	"	Left side, entered left lobe of liver; ball remains; died July 9, 1864. Buried in 3d Division grave yard, grave marked.
Wasson, Samuel	"	G	2d	"	Left lower jaw, entered one inch to left of symphasis, exit base, fracture jaw; sent to general hospital, July 10, 1864.
July 9, 1864.					
Idell, Thomas	"	A	"	"	Left leg, inner side of popliteal space, exit below and on opposite side of leg.
July 10, 1864.					
McKey, Niel	"	B	27th	"	Head, passing to left on line with sagittal suture, scalp wound; sent to general hospital July 15, 1864.
Kinney, Sylvester	"	E	"	"	Right thigh, entered two inches anterior to trochanter major, ball penetrated the trochanter, not extracted.
July 11, 1864.					
Epley, Thomas	"	G	17th	Artil.	Incised wound, right foot; sent to general hospital July 15, 1864.
July 12, 1864.					
Holton, Joseph	Cor.	E	8th	Ball.	Entered on inside of left leg, calf, exit direct line on outside; shot himself and to remain here till well sent to regiment August 8, 1864.
Rodman, Leonard	"	K	20th	Shell.	Contusion of abdomen gastronemia and left leg; sent to general hospital July 15, 1864.
July 13, 1864.					
Green, Wm. D.	Pr.	C	2d	Ball.	Neck, passing through ligamentum nuchae.

BATTLES AT AND NEAR PETERSBURG.—Continued.

Name.	Rank.	Co.	Regiment.	Missile.	Nature of Wound.
July 14, 1864.					
Tucker, C. H.	Pr.	B	27th Mich.	Shell.	Head, slight contusion, near superior angle of left parietal bone; sent to regiment July 25, 1864.
Miller, Campbell	Muscn.	I S. S.	"	"	Entrance left lumbar region, a large fragment penetrated cavity of abdomen and thorax, passing through obliquely up and forward, rested on ribs below and other side of nipple; died shortly after.
Anderson, Taron	Pr.	B	2d	Ball.	Entrance right nates, penetrating cavity of abdomen, ball remaining, mortal; died July 14, 1864.
July 15, 1864.					
Whittam, Richard	"	H	8th	"	Entered outer and upper third of left thigh, exit below on outside, penetrated inner anterior portion of middle third of right thigh, exit opposite hip; sent to general hospital July 17, 1864.
Hammond, George	"	C	27th	Shell.	Contusion, left breast, severe; sent to general hospital July 17, 1864.
Dunn, Wesley	Muscn.	K	"	Ball.	Left hip, entered two inches above and behind trochanter major ilium, fractured, small specula removed; ball not found.
Murtaugh, Ambrose	Pr.	I S. S.	"	Shell.	Contusion with laceration of left nates; sent to general hospital July 17, 1864.
Kent, William	"	K	"	Ball.	Metacarpal of second toe, left foot, fractured; sent to general hospital July 17, 1864
July 16, 1864.					
Riggs, Hurlbut	2d Lieut.	D	"	"	Left leg, anterior middle third, fracture of metacarpal, left hand ring finger metacarpal amputated; sent to general hospital July 17, 1864.
Messett, Charles	Pr.	B	8th	"	Grazed symphasis menti, extracted from right larynx.
July 17, 1864.					
Rule, James	"	"	27th	"	Lower third, right leg, entered inner side tibula, passing between the bones, exit directly opposite, tibula grazed; sent to general hospital July 17, '64.

Name	Rank	Co	Regt	Cause	Wound
Fowler, Thomas	1st Lieut.		1st Mich. S. S.		Entered left cheek, fractured malar bone, passing the parotid gland downward and backward, exit behind sterno cleido mastoid muscle.
July 18, 1864.					
Erwin, John T.	Pr.	B	2d Mich.		Left thigh, lower anterior third, flesh.
Granger, Leonard	"	D	20th "		Right shoulder and head, entered middle space of scapula, exit superior border of scapula, re-entered external to angle of lower jaw, course upward; extracted through the upper.
July 19, 1864.					
Bushey, John	"	B	27th "		Neck, entered right side, exit opposite, passing between ligamentum nuchæ; sent to general hospital July 25, 1864.
McDowel, George	"	1st Co	"	Shell.	Right arm, entered middle upper third of humerus, lacerating soft parts comminuting bone; amputated at surgical neck; sent to general hospital July 25, 1864.
Sayer, Jacob B.	"	G	"	"	Left shoulder, occipital, contusion, fracture of acromium process.
Clayton, Thomas	"	K	8th "	Per. cap	Left eye cornea injured.
July 20, 1864.					
McGraw, Frank	Cor.	H	2d "	Ball.	Left upper third, thigh; sent to general hospital July 22, 1864.
Casey, Thomas	"	C	"	"	Abdomen, three inches behind, entered superior spinal process of ilium, course upward and inward, penetrating abdomen, ilium fractured.
Kral, Thomas	Pr.	D	8th "	"	Left leg, entered one inch and anteriorly to inner tuberosity, head of tibia, course outward and downward, imbedded in tibia.
July 22, 1864.					
Meade, James	Sergt.	D	"	"	Thorax, entered upper and anterior portion of left lung; ball not found.
Stanley, Warren	Pr.	F	"	Spt. bl.	Left hip, glancing stroke, one inch behind head of femur.
Southerby, Wm.	"	E	2d "	"	Both hands, entered dorsum of left hand at phalangeal articulation of thumb, exit opposite touching middle finger, passing between metacarpals of ring and little fingers.
Briggs, Solomon	Sergt.	E	"	Shell.	Thorax, right side, contusion.

BATTLES AT AND NEAR PETERSBURG.—Continued.

Name.	Rank.	Co.	Regiment.	Missile.	Nature of Wound.
July 22, 1864.					
Norton, Walter	Pr.	C	27th Mich	Powder.	Face burnt by powder, explosion of shell.
July 23, 1864.					
Block, Frederick	"	H	" "	Ball.	Head, contused scalp outside and near left parietal eminence.
Todd, C. D.	1st Lieut.	E	17th "	"	Right arm, entered at insertion of deltoid, exit below and opposite.
Burley, Jerome	Pr.	F	27th "	"	Thorax, right side, entered one inch back of angle last true rib; extracted four inches back and below.
Smith, Wm.	"	E	2d "	"	Both thighs, outer side of upper middle third of right thigh, exit opposite, re-entered left thigh, exit outer side.
Russell, Joseph	"	G	27th "	"	Head, lacerating right anterior inferior angle of parietal bone, no apparent depression of bone.
Reynolds, Daniel	"	2 S. S.	" "	"	Left foot, third toe shattered; amputated.
July 24, 1864.					
Taylor, Henry	"	C	" "	Shell.	Left side lacerated, extending from anterior angle of scapula to three inches below the crest of ilium.
July 25, 1864.					
McCleand, John	"	K	2d "	"	Right arm, entered above inner condyle of humerus, exit middle of forearm, ulnar side.
Quantz, Albert	"	B	1st Mich. S. S.	"	Left leg, thigh.
Miller, Theodore	"	C	2d "	"	Back.
Percival, Wm.	"	F	27th "	"	Face.

July 27, 1864.					
Burns, Wm. H.	"	G	1st Mich. S. S.	Shell.	Right leg, fractured at knee joint; amputated leg.
Kightlinger, Geo.	Cor.	F	8th "	Ball.	Head, skull fractured, spicula removed and depression removed without trephining.
Owen, Warren	Pr.	K	2d "	Accdt.	Right ankle, dislocation of joint; reduced.
July 28, 1864.					
Little, George H.	Pr.	H	27th "	Ball.	Right foot, great toe.
July 29, 1864.					
Argyle, C. H.	"	B	2d "	"	Face, grazed.

Lieutenant Campbell.

Although a soldier, through constantly coming in contact with harassing scenes, becomes, in time, more or less hardened, still there are times when the more tender feelings of the heart are brought to the front.

I remember, after the death of Lieutenant T. Campbell, and his body had been taken from the hospital, his father (who was a clergyman in the southern part of this state—just where, I do not remember now), came to me and besought me to do all I possibly could to secure the body of his dear son, which it was his desire to take home to Michigan for interment. I deeply felt for the poor old gentleman, and, providing him a mount, I accompanied him to Army Headquarters, where permission was granted by the medical director that, providing the body was not in too advanced a state of decomposition, his request might be complied with. We readily found his boy, wrapped in a blanket, in that long trench marked today by the iron headboards provided by the United States of America. We soon procured a gun-box, in which the body was placed, sent in an ambulance to City Point and placed in the hands of an embalmer. I accompanied that afflicted father on his mission. Dr. Douglas, of New Jersey, was the accredited embalmer at City Point at that time, but when we arrived there we found decomposition had advanced to such an extent it was considered quite impossible to make the body presentable, and I advised the old gentleman to bury his son where thousands of his comrades were quietly sleeping, who had given their life's blood as freely as water to support the country and hold the stars and stripes aloft.

> The christian sage his sufferings bore,
> No murmur did he make,
> Well knowing the sacrifice he made
> Would yield a richer stake.

'Twas plain to all that Grant's attrition scheme would soon dispel the rebel hordes. We continued to carry important points, but met with no signal success. Lee still held the interior line, requiring a considerable less number of men than Grant.

Every day more or less wounded were brought in, who were duly cared for, and as soon as possible, forwarded to City Point, whence they were either shipped North, or discharged, according as the exigencies of the case demanded.

It looked to us as though Grant, by his tactics, resembled a "bull-dog," holding his enemy by the throat, exhausting and throttling him until the rebellion should die from asphyxiation or lack of the resources which gave him vitality.

Various movements were made by the army on both flanks up to July 30, when a mine was sprung in front of the Ninth Army Corps, which proved to be a miserable failure, thought it added to the long list of wounded. The following are the names:

BATTLES AT AND NEAR PETERSBURG.—Continued.

Name.	Rank.	Co.	Regiment.	Missile.	Nature of Wound.
July 30, 1864.					
Wright, W. B.	Lt. Col.	......	27th Mich.	Ball.	Neck, right side, passing backward and downward; ball remains.
Holden, S. S.	Capt.	K	20th "	"	Back and left hip, contusion.
Scofield, R. R.	"	1 S. S.	27th "	"	Back, contusion.
Moore, John S.	"	E	2d "	"	Left shoulder and head; trephined right frontal bone.
Burns, John H.	"	B	" "	"	Left shoulder, fracture of scapula.
Daniels, H. H.	Adjt.	"	" "	"	Left shoulder and left hip.
Buddach, Wm.	2d Lieut.	H	1st Mich. S. S.	"	Breast, contusion.
Hoffman, Allen	"	F	27th "	"	Left shoulder and chest.
Vickery, Richard	Ast. Sur.	......	2d "	Shell.	Upper third thigh ligature of left femoral artery.
Tucker, Charles	Pr.	B	27th "	Ball.	Left hand, severe.
McGouth, Oscar	Cor.	"	20th "	"	Left leg, calf, artery injured.
Fast, Henry W.	Pr.	G	" "	"	Right arm and right leg, contusion.
Cleveland, Geo.	"	B	27th "	"	Right wrist and right thigh; amputated lower third right arm.
Austin, W. S.	"	D	" "	"	Right arm; upper third amputated at shoulder joint.
Crouse, Joseph	"	H	" "	"	Face and left ear; exit near angle of mouth.
Fitch, E. N.	1st Sergt.	I	" "	"	Right foot and left leg, upper third; amputated right little toe and second toe.

BATTLES AT AND NEAR PETERSBURG.—Continued.

Names.	Rank.	Co.	Regiment.	Missile.	Nature of Wound.
July 30, 1864.					
Hoover, Conrad	Pr.	C	27th Mich.	Ball.	Back.
Paddock, Joseph	"	G	" "	"	Right arm.
St. John, Chas.	"	K	" "	"	Left leg.
Northrop, Wm.	"	H	1st Mich. S. S.	"	Right leg fractured.
Culver, Ed. D.	"	"	20th "	"	Left hip and nates.
Wagner, Adrian	"	D	8th "	"	Left upper third leg.
Nicholas, Joseph	"	E	1st Mich. S. S.	"	Left shoulder, passing downward.
Winfield, Nelson	"	2 S. S.	27th "	"	Hips.
Noyes, Oscar	"	"	" "	"	Left breast, penetrating.
Lausen, Matthias	"	"	" "	"	Left thigh, upper third.
Bohner, E.	"	A	2d "	"	Right shoulder.
Doud, Theodore	Sergt.	C	" "	Shell.	Right thigh, middle third; both thighs amputated; died August 1, 1864.
Christian, Wm.	"	G	8th "	"	Left arm, fracture.
Russell, John	Pr.	D	27th "	Ball.	Right leg, bone contusion; amputated at knee joint.
Gurney, Lemuel	"	F	" "	"	Face, grazed chin.
Barrich, Wm.	"	K	" "	"	Left thigh, upper third.
Dolph, Wm. D.	"	"	" "	"	Left leg.

Name	Rank	Co.	Regt.		Cause	Wound
McMahon, A. J.	"	D	"		Shell.	Head.
Sprague, R. A.	Cor.	B	2d		Ball.	Left side, contusion.
Webber, Samuel	Pr.	C	20th		"	Left forearm.
Vridenstine, Wm.	"	E	"		"	Right hand, index finger; amputated.
Winters, Peter	"	K	27th		Shell.	Head.
Ford, James	"	"	"		"	Head.
Bushnell, Henry	"	C	20th		Ball.	Back of hand shattered; metacarpal amputated.
Johnson, Rich. M.	"	10 S S	27th		"	Head, right parietal eminence.
Peck. Franklin		2 S. S.	"		Baynt.	Right forearm, accidental.
Lehman, Frederick	"	K	20th		Ball.	Face, not extracted.
Cleaveland, John	"	G	27th		Shell.	Head, slight.
Hazelton, Aaron	"	"	20th		"	Right thigh, contusion.
Fifield, Matthew	"	"	27th		Ball.	Left forearm.
Macomb, Peter	"	"	"		"	Right leg.
Bernice, Robt.	"	E	20th		Shell.	Right shoulder, slight.
Martin, Hurdus	"	C	27th		"	Face, flesh, slight.
Lombard, Jos.	"	H	"		"	Right hand, thumb and index finger.
Wagure, Louis	Cor.	B	"		"	Head, fracture, left parietal.
Hoover, Franklin	Pr.	D	"		Grape.	Right elbow, contusion.
Lewis, Wm. J.	"	C	20th		Ball.	Right shoulder, scapula.
Smith, George S.	"	I	"		"	Right breast and upper anterior side, right arm.

BATTLES AT AND NEAR PETERSBURG.—Continued.

Name.	Rank.	Co.	Regiment.	Missile.	Nature of Wound.
July 30, 1864.					
Karr, Philander	Cor.	I	8th Mich	Ball.	Left hand; amputated middle finger.
Dakers, Stephen	Sergt.	"	2d "	"	Left arm.
Crandell, Marshal	"	D	" "	"	Right hand, index and second fingers.
Crysler, Marcus	Pr.	B	20th "	"	Left hip.
Brevoort, John N	"	C	8th "	Shell.	Right leg, slight.
Taylor, Eugene	"	"	1st Mich. S. S.	Ball.	Face, both cheeks, severe.
Ellis, A. J	"	H	" "	"	Right leg, bone fractured.
Crandell, Solon	"	G	17th Mich	"	Left ankle.
Collin, Jacob	"	K	1st Mich. S. S.	Shell.	Left arm, fracture.
Fishepel, Gabriel	"	C	27th "	"	Left side.
Crandell, George E	"	F	20th "	Ball.	Right upper third leg, flesh.
Brant, Charles	"	D	8th "	"	Head, slight; returned to regiment August 8, 1864.
Thomas, John	"	B	27th "	"	Left leg.
Tresise, Wm	Sergt.	C	" "	Ball.	Neck and shoulder, entered right side of neck passing backward and downward; ball removed.
Albert, George	Pr.	A	" "	"	Left side and left knee; amputated left lower third femur.
Vanwite, Hugh	"	D	" "	"	Left Hip.
Bruen, John	"	F	" "	"	Right upper leg; amputated upper third.

THE GREAT REBELLION.

Name	Rank	Co.				Injury
Smith, Charles	"	B	"			Left foot.
Deboe, Jacob	Sergt.	D	8th	"	"	Left hand, flesh.
Rich, Henry	Pr.	K	27th	"	"	Abdomen.
McClellan, Howard	"	A	"	"	"	Left arm, upper third.
Walker, S. G.	Sergt.	B	1st Mich. S. S.		Shell.	Right hand, phalange of index finger.
Noyes, Kirke W.	"	D	"		Ball.	Right foot, slight.
Ott, Alpheus	Cor.	I	8th	"	"	Right upper third thigh.
Noll, Conrad	Pr.	D	20th	"	"	Left upper third thigh.
Georgia, Washington	Cor.	G	2d	"	"	Left forearm, contusion.
Crosberry, Henry	Pr.	D	27th	"	"	Neck.
Showy, John	"	C	2d	"	Shell.	Right foot.
Maber, William O.	"	E	27th	"	Ball.	Right abdomen and both thighs.
Mount, Richard	"	G	20th	"	Shell.	Left nates, contusion.
Chadwick, W. H.	Sergt.	C	"	"	"	Face, ramus, left jaw.
Hurlburt, Nehemiah L.	Pr.	1 S. S.	27th	"	"	Both legs, contusion.
Mills, Charles	"	H	"	"	"	Left leg; amputated below knee.
Cole, Charles	"	I	"	"	"	Left shoulder; ball extracted.
Rose, Aaron	"	K	"	"	"	Head slight, left shoulder; ball extracted.
Dunn, Richard	Cor.	G	2d	"	"	Left forearm, contusion.
Kinney, John J.	"	1 S. S.	27th	"	Shell.	Left thigh.
Ramsey, James W.	"	D	"	"	Ball.	Right arm.

BATTLES AT AND NEAR PETERSBURG.—Continued.

Name.	Rank.	Co.	Regiment.	Missile.	Nature of Wound.
July 30, 1864.					
Beardsley, Daniel	Pr.	F	20th Mich	Shell.	{ Right arm lacerated and fracture of humerus; amputated upper third.
Lockwood, James	"	K	" "	"	Abdomen, severe.
Goodridge, Edgar	"	B	" "	Ball.	Left leg, slight.
Hummel, Henry	Cor.	H	2d "	Shell.	Right leg fractured; amputated upper third.
Carpenter, Watson W.	Pr.	F	20th "	Ball.	Left thigh, severe.
McIntyre, Hugh A.	Cor.	K	" "	"	Right hand, third and fourth fingers shattered.
Bohn, Jacob	"	H	8th "	Shell.	Head, left side.
Tillotson, Asa	Pr.	E	2d "	Ball.	Abdomen, severe.
Wood, Henry	"	G	20th "		Sprain, right foot.
Densmore, Wm.	"	E	27th "	Shell.	Right shoulder, slight.
Parks, Myron C.	Cor.	F	20th "	"	Carried away left leg; died August 1, 1864.
Show, Edwin P.	Pr.	"	1st Mich. S. S.	"	Right arm.
July 31, 1864.					
Moore, Wm. H.	"	G	2d "	Ball.	Left thigh, lower third.
Aug. 1, 1864.					
Bates, Charles S.	"	"	27th "	"	Left hip, above and in front of trochanters.

THE GREAT REBELLION.   141

Date / Name	Rank	Co.	Regiment		Wound	Description
Aug. 2, 1864.						
Lafarge, Henry F	"	B	20th "		"	Right thigh, middle third anterior aspect; ball remained.
Wilkinson, Andy	"	I	8th "		"	Head, entering between left mastoid process and occipital protuberance; died August 3, 1864.
Aug. 3, 1864.						
Fair, Alexander	"	G	27th "		"	Head, scalp, on line of sagittal suture.
Foot, George W	"	"	8th "		"	Face, entered right of symphasis, course downward and backward.
Aug. 5, 1864.						
Flsk, George L	"	B	17th "		Htch.	Right foot, incised great toe.
Aldrich, David	"	"	2d "		Ball.	Left thigh, upper third, entered two inches below and in front trochanter major; ball imbedded in femur.
Wheelan, A. F	Surgeon.		1st Mich. S. S.		Shell.	Right leg, contusion, thigh.
Aug. 11, 1864.						
Sloan, George	Pr.	C	27th "		Ball.	Head, entered behind right mastold, exit right orbit; died August 13, 1864.
Aug. 12, 1864.						
Welsh, Daniel A	"	"	8th "		"	Head, right temple grazed.
Aug. 14, 1864.						
Fox, Myron J	"	I	1st Mich. S. S.		"	Right thigh, grazed lower third.
McKiver, Neil	"	C	2d "		"	Right hand fingers, index and second fingers.
Aug. 15, 1864.						
McKeel, Oscar	"	"	1st Mich. S. S.		"	Head, along line of sagittal suture.
Aug. 16, 1864.						
Fetetes, Charles	Cor.	K	2d "		Ball.	Thorax grazed, slightly denuding ribs; ball dropped out.

BATTLES AT AND NEAR PETERSBURG.—*Continued.*

Name.	Rank.	Co.	Regiment.	Missile.	Nature of Wound.
Aug. 17, 1864.					
Cain, Noah	Pr.	G	1st Mich. S. S.	Ball.	Abdomen, entered two inches above umbilicus, exit left lumbar region penetrating cavity; dead.
Aug. 18, 1864.					
Spears, Thomas	Sergt.	H	20th "	Shell.	Left thigh, contusion.

Among the many wounded was one whose services were missed more than words can tell in our hospital.

Richard Vickery, Assistant Surgeon of the 2d Michigan Infantry, always on duty to the front, received a severe wound, perforating the femoral artery, which, when he was brought to the hospital he asked me to ligate. I performed that service for my friend to the best of my ability, and am very glad to know today that, although his recovery was very protracted, yet his services were so much appreciated by the medical department that he was appointed surgeon in the regular army. Since the doctor's recovery I have received several letters from him, one from Ireland, and three or four from western points where he has been stationed, which has given me much pleasure.

Dr. Vickery was a graduate of the university of Michigan. An Irishman by birth, he left his home (Skibberdeen) for America early in life and ever remained true to and shedding his blood willingly for his adopted country.

The Weldon Railroad furnished to Lee's army up to this date its principal supplies of food, clothing and ammunition, hence the desire of our general-in-chief to destroy it. He, therefore, ordered Warren with his Fifth Corps, on the 16th of August, to seize it, which he did some eight miles south of Petersburg.

The enemy could illy spare that road, and hastened their troops forward to that point to drive Warren back and retake it.

The Ninth Corps, which was stationed in front of Petersburg, was rushed, under Park, to the aid of Warren. My hospital train accompanied it, and reached the point assigned us not far from noon on the 19th. I remember, as we lay there taking our coffee, the terrific charge of the rebels, which, although it greatly surprised did not demoralize the troops.

Although quite a number of shells were scattered among us, there was comparatively little damage done, destroying two or three ambulances, killing a few horses and mortally wounding a surgeon of one of the New York regiments. It was fortunate for Warren that the Ninth Corps was at hand at that time, or the Fifth Corps must have been captured or destroyed. General O. B. Wilcox, who commanded our division, quickly reinforced Warren, but with no small loss, as the names of the following wounded will show:

BATTLE OF WELDON RAILROAD.

Name.	Rank.	Co.	Regiment.	Missile.	Nature of Wound.
Aug. 19, 1864.					
Clark, Elmer	Pr.	D	27th Mich.	Ball.	Right thigh.
Demond, Wm	Cor.	F	8th "	"	Left forearm.
McKilver, Wm	Sergt.	H	27th "	"	Right leg, through thorax.
Perkins, G. W.	Pr.	G	8th "	"	Left forearm; amputated at lower third.
Frank, Howe	"	"	20th "	"	Left thigh, fractured; amputated middle third.
Drews, Frederick	"	B	8th "	"	Left side of head.
Chamberlain, H. B.	Capt.	I	27th "	"	Right forearm.
Sawyer, B. F.	Pr.	G	8th "	"	Right thorax.
Clark, Henry	2d Lieut.	H	" "	"	Left forearm.
Gillis, Andrew	Sergt.	A	" "	"	Right foot.
Webster, Lewis	"	"	" "	"	Right hand.
Sumner, John	Capt.	D	" "	"	Right nates.
Hendee Oscar P.	Lieut.	F	" "	"	Right forearm.
Walker, Moses	Pr.	A	" "	"	Left leg; amputated.
Bachus, Wm	Cor.	C	27th "	"	Left shoulder.
Nash, D. L.	Pr.	H	2d "	"	Contusion, breast.

BATTLE OF WELDON RAILROAD.—Continued.

Name.	Rank.	Co.	Regiment.	Missile.	Nature of Wound.
Aug. 19, 1864.					
Neely, Daniel	"	"	8th "	"	Right leg, flesh.
Goodman, D. R.	Cor.	"	" "	"	Right thigh, flesh.
Minicher	Pr.	A	8th "	"	Left arm and abdomen; dead.
Hanay	Lieut.		" "	"	Right forearm; amputated upper third.
Leonard, Fred	Cor.	A	2d "	"	Right hand; imbedded in ball of thumb.
Crawford, M. A.	"	E	8th "	"	Right arm, flesh.
Aug. 27, 1864.					
Stenegar, Milton	Pr.	B	27th "	Sld Shot	Right shoulder, contusion.
Wheeler, W. C.	"	H	8th "	Ball.	Head, scalp.
Minhen, Andrew	"	F	27th "	"	Right leg.
Aug. 22, 1864.					
Kniffen, John J	"	B	8th "	"	Right shoulder, contusion.
Pratt, William	2d Lieut.	I	27th "	"	Right thigh, contusion.
Aug. 24, 1864.					
Gillis, A. H	Pr.	A	8th "	"	Right, flesh, slight.
Sept. 19, 1864.					
Bird, Henry	"	2 S. S.	27th "	"	Right foot, slight.

Sept. 30, 1864.					
McCormith, G. H.	"	E	8th	"	Left leg.
Isaac, Kidney	"	G	"	"	Abdomen, mortal; died September 30, 1864.
Palmer, Lavant	"	B	2d	"	Right leg.
Poal, John M.	"	C	27th	"	Right arm.
Anderson, James	"	K	2d	"	Left leg.
Meade, T. S.	1st Lieut.	I S. S.	27th	"	Right side, penetrating lung; ball not found.
Kanard, H.	Sergt.	F	2d	"	Right leg.
O'Niel, Edward	Pr.	B	20th	"	Head, scalp wound.
Clark, Wm.	"	C	2d	"	Left thigh, contusion.
Ritchley, Lyman W.	"	K	8th	"	Left thigh.
Rendel, Wm.	"	"	2d	"	Right leg.
McComas, D. H.	"	E	8th	"	Right leg, fractured; amputated middle third.
Bird, Elijah	"	A	"	"	Left leg, fractured; amputated lower third.
Oct. 1, 1864.					
Potter, John W.	Cor.	C	1st Mich. S. S.	"	Left foot fracture, metacarpus; ball extracted.
Martin, James	Pr.	D	27th Mich.	"	Head, jaw fractured; spicula removed.
Oct. 2, 1864.					
Byron, James	Pr.	D	27th Mich.	Ball.	Left arm, radius fractured, spicula removed.
Oct. 3, 1864.					
Hyllard, B. E.	"	K	"	"	Left arm.

BATTLE OF WELDON RAILROAD.—*Continued.*

Name.	Rank.	Co.	Regiment.	Missile.	Nature of Wound.
Oct. 3, 1864.					
Smith, G. S.	"	"	" "	Ramrod.	Right hand penetrated.
Oct. 4, 1864.					
Chapin, Marshal	Sergt.	"	8th "	Ball.	Right thigh; ball not found.
Gordon, James	Pr.	E	" "	"	Right hand finger, second finger; second phalange amputated.
Oct. 8, 1864.					
Russell, L. W.	"	C	2d "	"	Left arm, fracture; amputated middle third arm.
Oct. 27, 1864.					
Marshall, Wm.	"	D	" "	"	Right hand, forefinger; amputated.
Truman, Frederick	"	A	" "	"	Left thigh.
Harris, Charles	"	H	1st Mich.S.S.	"	Back and thigh; entered cavity of thorax; died November 12, 1864.

MAJOR HORATIO BELCHER,
8th Michigan Infantry.

One of the more prominent losses which we sustained that day was Major Horatio Belcher, who·was, I believe, one of the bravest men of the old 8th, for it is a fact that it was an utter impossibility for him to keep out of a fight. He had been wounded in East Tennessee the fall before, and seriously at Cold Harbor on the 3d of June, and it certainly appeared as though he led a charmed life. After the rebels were repulsed he was brought to me terribly shot to pieces, bearing five wounds, any of which was sufficient to prove mortal. He was a native of Flint, where his family resided for many years. We placed the body in as presentable a condition as possible, and forwarded it to his friends in Michigan.

The balance of the summer and fall of 1864 was, as before implied, a mere "bull-dog," lying-in-wait sort of a game.

On October 27, 1864, an effort was made by General Grant to again break Lee's right at Poplar Grove Church. He was successful in that the rebels were compelled to fall back over a mile and a half to their inner line of works, Grant succeeding in further tightening his grip and preventing the escape of the Army of Northern Virginia for the winter of 1864-65.

The following are the names of those wounded in this encounter:

BATTLE OF POPLAR GROVE CHURCH.

Name.	Rank.	Co.	Regiment.	Missile.	Nature of Wound.
Stage, Suge	Pr.	H	2d Mich.	Ball.	Right knee, flesh.
Leonard, Henry	"	A	" "	"	Left thigh, flesh.
Sawyer, Jacob B.	"	G	27th "	"	Head, frontal bone, serious.
Fletcher, Robt.	"	A	1st Mich, S. S.	"	Head, flesh.
McGiven, John	"	E	" "	"	Left hand contused.
Thomas, John	"	I	" "	"	Left leg contused.
Lee, George	"	F	2d "	"	Neck, flesh.
Oct. 28, 1864.					
Shattuck, Nelson	"	"	5th "		Right shoulder.
Monroe, D. S.	Cor.	H	20th "		Occipital; ball extracted.
Chambers, Jas.	Pr.	F	27th "		Left hand; amputated lower third arm.

The presidential election which occurred in November occupied largely the attention of the troops.

The Army of the Potomac, up to this date, had secured no signal results. The people of the North seemed to have settled down in despair. Resolutions at various political conventions were passed that the war thus far was a failure, and despondency was everywhere prevalent until the Baltimore Convention which unanimously renominated Mr. Lincoln.

It will be remembered that President Lincoln had issued on Monday, the 22d of September, 1862, the famous Proclamation of Emancipation, and that, up to this date, it seemed to have been a dead letter; but Abraham Lincoln had faith to believe that "all men *should* stand and *would* stand equal before the law," be they black or white. That his memorable words may be presented to all Americans wherever they may be, who read this volume, I will insert it here:

"I, Abraham Lincoln, President of the United States of America and Commander-in-Chief of the Army and Navy thereof, do hereby proclaim and declare that hereafter, as heretofore, the war will be prosecuted for the object of practically restoring to the Constitutional relation between the United States and each of the States and the people thereof in which States that relation is or may be suspended or disturbed.

"That it is my purpose upon the next meeting of Congress to again recommend the adoption of a practical measure tendering pecuniary aid to the free acceptance or rejection of all slave States, so-called, the people whereof may not then be in rebellion against the United States, and which States may then have voluntarily adopted, or thereafter may voluntarily adopt, immediate or gradual abolition of slavery within their respective limits, and their efforts to colonize persons of African descent with their consent upon this continent or elsewhere with the previously obtained consent of the government existing there will be continued.

"That on the 1st day of January, in the year of our Lord 1863, all persons held as slaves in any State or designated part of a State, whereof the people shall be in rebellion against the United States, shall be then, thenceforward and FOREVER FREE; and the Executive Government of the United States, including the Military and Naval authority thereof, will recognize and maintain the freedom of such persons and will do no act or acts to repress such persons or any of them in any efforts they may make for their actual freedom.

"That the Executive will, on the 1st of January aforesaid, by proclamation, designate the States and parts of States, if any, in which the people thereof respectively shall then be in rebellion against the United States. And the fact that any State or the people thereof shall on that day be in good faith represented in the Congress of the United States by members chosen thereto at elections wherein the majority of the qualified voters of such State shall have participated, shall, in the absence of strong countervailing testimony, be deemed conclusive evidence that such State and the people thereof are not then in rebellion against the United States."

The premises laid down in the foregoing by President Lincoln gave all parties to understand that cost what it may, and in the teeth of the fact that a general gloom pervaded the national atmosphere, the Constitution formed by the FATHERS must, at *every* sacrifice, be preserved though every drop of blood floating in the veins of the free North be shed.

These momentous questions were discussed in cabinet meetings, as they were in every part of the country, daily.

SLAVERY was ABOLISHED; the edict had gone forth that all men possessed certain inalienable rights as asserted by the FATHERS, namely: To LIFE, LIBERTY AND THE PURSUIT OF HAPPINESS.

The Gordian knot was now cut, the Ship of State was now well out to sea.

Lincoln, the nominee of the party, determined to prosecute the war to its legitimate conclusions.

Fremont, the sorehead, and McClellan, a disappointed and insufficient military leader, which experience had taught us after the expenditure of over a billion of dollars, had neither the pluck, energy nor genius to meet the exigencies of the case.

The 4th of November, 1864, was an ever-memorable day in the annals of the republic, and taught (by the re-election of Lincoln) our trans-Atlantic as well as our internal foes that there was a fixed and indomitable determination to maintain the integrity of the American Union. That our national anthem, written on the surrender of Cornwallis, was no idle song, but like the "Marseilles Hymn" and "God Save the Queen," meant more than rebels could destroy.

"Star spangled banner, long may she wave
O'er the home of the free and the land of the brave."

Four millions of human beings had been held, heretofore, in the most abject slavery, which had brought into derision the proclamation made July 4, 1776.

The world had laughed at the Starry Banner and called it a living lie.

The Wesleys, as they preached the gospel of *British freedom*, said our system was the "sum of all villainies."

The midnight gloom, which then o'erspread us,
Made brighter than the "Orion" light
The morn that quickly dawned upon us.

After the result of the election was known, and Sherman had well advanced with the southern wing of the Grand Armies toward Savannah, it became apparent that this republic was not ephemeral. As the contending armies rapidly advanced from point to point in the great death struggle it became apparent to all the world that slavery on this continent was doomed, and that no flag, no stars and *bars*, no Austrian duke or other crowned head, could exist and rule upon this continent. The Stars and Stripes, the Red, the White and the Blue *alone* should cast its proud folds to the breeze in this country.

The winter of 1864-65 was characterized with the deepest anxiety by all the belligerent forces. Constant shelling was kept up almost day and night upon both sides.

Our old first division occupied the right of the line, and details of our men on vidette and picket duty were extremely severe, as will be seen by the list of wounded, whose names are as follows:

WOUNDED WHILE ON PICKET DUTY IN FRONT OF PETERSBURG.

Name.	Rank.	Co.	Regiment.	Missile.	Nature of Wound.
Dec. 5, 1864.					
Burns, Wm. H.	Pr.	G	1st Mich. S. S.	Shell.	Right leg, knee joint; amputated leg.
McCole, John C.	"	B	" "	"	Right leg, flesh.
Kightlinger, Geo.	Cor.	F	8th "	Ball.	Head, skull fractured, spicula removed; died at City Point.
Dec. 6, 1864.					
Patterson, J. Q.	Lieut.		27th "	"	Left arm and side, entered arm, penetrating side and passing out of back.
Dec. 13, 1864.					
McEwing, Henry	Pr.	D	20th "	"	Head, right temple, lodging back of orbit destroying orbital nerve.
Dec. 14, 1864.					
Field, H. C.	Cor.	C	1st Mich. S. S.	"	Head, flesh, slight.
Dec. 15, 1864.					
Houghtelling, H.	Pr.	B	8th Mich.	"	Right arm, flesh; ball extracted.
Dec. 19, 1864.					
Nelson, Launt	"	I	" "	Burnt.	Face; powder burn.
Dec. 22, 1864.					
Belt, Maurice	"	B	27th "	Ball.	Head, flesh.
Dec. 23, 1864.					
Carpenter, Hemen	Sergt.	E	20th "	"	Right shoulder, flesh.

WOUNDED AT FALL OF PETERSBURG, FROM MARCH 25 TO APRIL 2, 1865.

Name.	Rank.	Co.	Regiment.	Missile.	Nature of Wound.
Dahew, Steven	Lieut.		2d Mich.	Ball.	Right arm; sent to City Point.
Fish, D. R.	Adjt.		" "	"	Left thigh; sent to City Point.
Hule, Lemuel W.	Pr.	A	20th "	"	Left hand; sent to City Point.
Shaffer, Wm.	"	E	" "	"	Head, flesh; sent to City Point.
Hammond, Chas.	Sergt.	E	" "	"	Shoulder and neck; sent to City Point.
Curtis, I. L.	Pr.	G	2d "	"	Groin, flesh; sent to City Point.
Lutz, Christian C.	"	K	20th "	"	Right side, flesh; sent to City Point.
Webster, Brayton G.	"	F	" "	"	Left elbow; amputated lower third; sent to City Point.
Belner, Edward	"	H	2d "	"	Nates; sent to City Point.
McCollister, Jas.	"	E	20th "	"	Left arm; sent to City Point.
Everson, Chas.	"	A	2d "	Shell.	Right leg; cent to City Point.
Rothchild, Levi	"	I	" "	Ball.	Head; died March 26, 1865.
Falcon, Fred	"	B	1st Mich. S. S.	"	Left eye; sent to general hospital.
Haven , Wm.	"	F	2d Mich.	"	Right hand; sent to general hospital.
Rogers, Wm.	"	C	" "	"	Left leg; sent to general hospital.
March 29, 1865.					
Weisel, Thos.	"	K	1st Mich. S.S.	"	Face, severe; sent to general hospital.

Name	Rank	Co.	Regt.	Cause	Wound
Chapman, Oscar B.	"	B	20th "		Shell.	Neck, slight; sent to general hospital.
Allen, Samuel	"	D	" "		Ball.	Left eye, ball extracted; sent to general hospital.
Doty, Zebulon	"	I	" "		"	Mouth; sent to general hospital.
Bourn, Wm.	"	H	8th "		"	Left arm; sent to general hospital.
April 1, 1865.						
Wetherbee, W. A.	"	B	2d "		"	Left foot, fracture; amputated third toe; supposed to be self-mutilation.
Allen, James	"	"	" "		"	Left foot, fracture; amputated second toe; supposed to be self-mutilation.
April 2, 1865.						
Fales, Porter	"	G	1st Mich. S. S.		"	Right hand, fracture; amputated three fingers.
Nichols, Asbel W.	Lt. Col.		" "		"	Left side, not penetrating; ball removed.
Fry, George	Pr.		" "		"	Inferior maxillary; part of maxillary carried away.
Burritt, Henry	2d Lieut.	D	8th "		"	Left arm.
Brown, George	Pr.	G	" "		"	Left hand; little finger amputated.
Moynahan, Jas.	1st Lieut.	D	27th "		"	Left arm.
King, Ransom	Pr.	A	8th "		Shell.	Left leg.
Sage, Wesley M.	"	C	1st Mich. S. S.		"	Head.
Sawyer, Andrew J.	"	"	" "		"	Scalp.
Holton, Joseph E.	Cor.	E	8th Mich.		"	Left thigh.
Chapman, Geo.	Pr.	C	" "		"	Left hand, middle fingers.
Watson, David	"	D	1st Mich. S. S.		"	Right thigh.
Deland, I. S.	Capt.	K	" "		"	Left arm.

FALL OF PETERSBURG.—Continued.

Name.	Rank.	Co.	Regiment.	Missile.	Nature of Wound.
April 2, 1865.					
Lombart, James	Pr.	H	27th Mich.	Shell.	Head, scalp.
Souls, F. D.	1st Lieut.	B	1st Mich. S. S.	"	Left leg.
Freeman, Lutton	Pr.	K	" "	"	Left thigh.
Parker, Cephas C.	Cor.	G	" "	"	Right thigh.
Hall, Cornelius	Pr.	K	" "	"	Right arm.
Gunther, Jacob	"	"	" "	"	Left thigh.
Jackson, S. D.	"	D	2d "	"	Left thigh.
Mitchell, Wm.	"	E	1st Mich. S. S.	"	Right thigh.
Farley, William	"	"	8th "	"	Right thigh.
Price, William	"	H	1st Mich. S. S.	"	Left thigh.
Hiller, R. M.	"	B	2d "	"	Right hand, fingers.
Camboll, Richard	Sergt.	I	1st Mich. S. S.	"	Left shoulder joint.
Henland, H. H.	1st Lieut.	G	" "	"	Head, face.
Brevoort, John A.	Pr.	C	8th "	"	Right leg.
Gee, Wm. F.	"	B	" "	"	Head.
Miller, George	Cor.	I S. S.	27th "	"	Left hand.
Chambers, Robt.	Pr.	C	" "	"	Chest, not penetrating.

At this period I had become, by the sickness and resignation of Surgeon Bonine, Surgeon-in-Chief of the Field Hospital of the First Division of the Ninth Army Corps. The duties at that time were extremely oppressive, and whether they were well discharged or not our comrades must decide. Such a position is weighted with responsibilities which are utterly impossible for any one to appreciate except those who have labored in that capacity.

The atmosphere in that part of the country was cold and damp in the extreme and all the debilitating influences that beset soldiers in active campaign prevailed. It was no uncommon thing to find at each morning roll-call from one hundred to five hundred men suffering from disease and wounds in our tents.

I pause right here to thank my staff for their never-failing and hearty support which I ever received from them during that trying winter. My First Assistant Surgeon, Dr. Aaron Vanderveen, now living in Grand Haven, Mich., responded faithfully to every requirement asked of him. To Dr. Fitch of the 79th New York, and Dr. W. E. Sherlock of the 51st Pennsylvania, I am under lasting obligations, as well as to other gentlemen who did excellent service until the spring campaign of the following year.

During the winter of 1864-65 the armies in front of Petersburg were comparatively inactive, making flank movements to Deep Bottoms on the right, the Weldon Railroad and Hatcher's Run on the left, which movements were undoubtedly made by the General-in-Chief to prevent the escape of the rebel army from the front of Richmond and Petersburg.

There can be no question but that General Lee now began to realize that the "bull-dog grip" had become so tightened that the day of doom could not much longer be deferred.

Sheridan had now destroyed the Shenandoah Valley, and the resources of the enemy for the sustenance of a large army were effectually destroyed.

Early had been taught from Fisher's Hill a lesson that though the boys in blue might have been caught napping, the great vital resources yet unexpended by the North would, like a cyclone following a clear sun, rain down and destroy their every hope of success in this fratricidal war.

Sherman's campaign in the Southern Department convinced Lee in front of Petersburg that the hope of establishing a Southern Confederacy was futile.

Mr. Lincoln sat in the White House anxiously awaiting news from the front.

The nation, in January 1865, seemed to pause, and, as it were, hold its breath. In fact a general paralysis had seized everything in all parts of the country. Either the rebellion was in the last ditch or the States at war with each other must consent to a compromise.

While all were on the tiptoe of expectation, wondering what would come next, one cold, dreary morning in February (3d), 1865, Alexander H. Stevens, J. H. Campbell, and R. M. T. Hunter, representing the rebel confederacy, were passed through our lines desiring an interview with General Grant. They were admitted and conducted to City Point, placed upon a steamer, and sent to Hampden Roads.

So far as my military knowledge is concerned, I am impressed the General had no desire to hold any parley as to the political status of the war, but felt that his responsibilities related simply to the military conduct of affairs. The rebel emissaries were, therefore, placed by him upon the "River Queen," and the President notified to that effect.

Mr. Seward, then Secretary of State for the United States, was despatched from Washington to ascertain the object of their visit, and the President consented to become a party to the interview. The Emancipation Proclamation had been given to the world and he had expressed to many delegations a positive determination not to recede therefrom. Hence the only terms upon which peace could be concluded must be based upon the terms expressed in that proclamation. Many questions were discussed by those gentlemen on the "River Queen" on that eventful day, but nothing was allowed by the President to be considered which should in anywise abrogate the Proclamation of Freedom which he had promulgated.

The rebel emissaries were curious to know what the status of freedmen should be. Should they hold the right of franchise? asked Campbell. They are ignorant! They know nothing of the rights of free men! And right at this point the climax was reached.

The great Lincoln, who was ordained by an allwise Providence to answer this question, after considering for over an hour, and Stevens, Hunter, Campbell and Seward apparently holding their breath in anticipation of the words that should come from that great hero's lips, gave them an answer such as a child could comprehend, but fraught with such power that it drove the truth home to the hearts of all true loyal lovers of liberty be they black or white. That hour of silence must have been profound, and as I have studied the great epochs |which have occurred in the history of the civilized world from which I have been able to learn, the fact seems pregnant that the God of right, the God of justice, the God of heaven had placed his hand upon the man to answer this question as a fiat going, forth from His eternal throne. A question that had disturbed the peace of the world for hundreds of years was solved by the relating of a homely Illinois story which runs as follows:

"This question reminds me of a man out in Illinois by the name of Case who undertook, a few years ago, to raise a very large herd of hogs. It was a great trouble to feed them, and how to get around this was a great puzzle to him. At length he hit upon the plan of planting an immense field of potatoes, and, when they were sufficiently grown, 'he♦ turned the whole herd into the field and let them have full swing, thus saving not only the labor of feeding the hogs, but that, also, of digging the potatoes.

"Charmed with his sagacity, he stood one day leaning against the fence counting the hogs, when a neighbor came along. 'Well, well,'

said he, 'Mr. Case, this is all very fine! Your hogs are doing very well just now, but you know out here in Illinois the frost comes early and the ground freezes a foot deep. Then what are they going to do?'
"This was a view of the matter which Mr. Case had not taken into account. Butchering time for hogs was away in December or January. He scratched his head and at length stammered :
"'Well, it may come pretty hard on their *snouts*, but I dont see but it will be *root hog or die.*'"
The question of American franchise, the doctrine that all men should stand equal before the law was now solved. The great fact was shown to be true that no matter what the color or what the nationality might be, native born or naturalized, whoever dwelt in these States was entitled by our Constitution to *rights*, to *privileges* and *immunities* of which he should not be deprived except by due process of law.

BRITAIN'S PREMIER, DISRAELI.

History does not record that Stevens, Campbell and Hunter were not empowered by the Richmond government to conclude a peace without the South retaining their slaves. And so far as we know today it was a fixed determination, should peace be obtained outside of a perfect defeat of the rebel armies, it should be on no other basis than that the rebels should *retain* the *institution* of *slavery*.

The great fact and fixed determination of the North had been decided that we would wash, if need be, by a baptism of blood the stain of slavery from our escutcheon.

Russia had the year before, by an edict of Alexander II, abolished her serfdom.

Great Britain, by her Premier Disraeli, had declared to the world that whoever trod British soil were freemen. How could the Great Republic do less than at least take the same platform, if not advance beyond the principles of these monarchial governments?

The morning dawn of a more glorious day was now beaming on the world. Every reader of history can but concur with me in saying:

> The light of life, hereto, had been but dim,
> The darkness, heretofore so bleak, so glim,
> The nations had o'erpowered, was burst;
> A larger liberty, the heir to which we all were born.
> The legacy the God of Heaven ordained for men,
> Should ne'er be now withheld.

Pennsylvania, at this date, supplied a large division to our Army Corps, which was placed under General Hartranft and attached to ours, now under command of Major General Park.

Those Pennsylvanians came to us about the latter end of February, 1865. As near as I could judge they must have been recruited from miners and farmers of that State. I remember they were encamped about a quarter of a mile in front of the field hospital of which I had charge. They had had no military experience, never having been under fire, and were illy prepared for what they were, right early in their service, compelled to endure.

The "bull-dog" grip which Grant had fastened upon the rebel throat had convinced its leader that something must be done, and so he ordered the best corps in his army to break our lines. General Gordon was probably the best prepared of any of his lieutenants to make the venture.

Fort Stedman was an earthwork commanding the inner line, occupied by the Ninth Army Corps, to the rear of which those Pennsylvanians were encamped.

General Hartranft had been with us as Colonel of the 51st Pennsylvania, and had commanded the first brigade of our division through several hard fought battles, namely: Second Bull Run,

Antietam, Chantilly, Ironworks, South Mountain, with Grant at Vicksburg, and through our East Tennessee campaign, up to the present time Perhaps, without disparagement to any other officer, I may be allowed to say he was the pride of our corps. He stood about six feet, well proportioned, the perfect embodiment of what I conceive to be a soldier, not excepting even his morale.

When Gordon, at the command of Lee, made that dash upon Fort Stedman, Hartranft, riding on his white horse in front of his division, exclaimed: "Pennsylvanians, the time has come for you to do your duty." The two old divisions of our corps reinforced him rapidly and there followed a sharp and desperate encounter. Although Hartranft himself escaped he left fully three-fourths of those one hundred days' men lying in that bloody gorge. The long trench filled with those poor fellows, placed four deep, wrapped in their blankets, bore sad testimony to the fact that they had nobly responded to their General's call and done all they could —"their duty."

Gordon was repulsed and the rebel army had now no hope of escape, and the fear of our General (that some morning we should awake to find the enemy gone), was dispelled.

President Lincoln, after continuous consultation with the Secretary of War (through whom reports were constantly received), came to City Point and made his home on board the "River Queen," anchored off in the James River, so that he might be in constant communication with the General-in-Chief, and if by any word he could say, any encouragement he could give, contribute to the suppression of the rebellion which it would seem was now well under control.

It will be remembered that the campaign of Shenandoah Valley, under Sheridan, was a pronounced success, and there was no more hope in that quarter for the rebels. Harper's Ferry, heretofore having been the principal arsenal in that section of the country was restored to the Union. The Valley of the Shenandoah will forever remain historic in the history of the nation as having been characterized with more sacrifices than had been made in any other part of the country where the contending armies had operated. I opine, had not Sheridan succeeded in depleting the resources of our enemies in that direction, the war of the rebellion would have lasted at least two or three years longer than it did. The foresight of our Lieutenant General was now apparent. The War Department seemed to have had the impression that West Point, birth and other considerations should be taken into account in the workings of those days. But the genius of the man developed as the occasion called for it. Sheridan was a young man, pale, slim, and sickly, but he possessed those inherent qualities which characterized some of the great cavalry officers of NAPOLEON BONAPARTE. I remember noticing him on one occasion at Berksville, as he rode past my hospital train on his black horse, "Rienzi," how pale and feeble he looked. It hardly seemed possible that such a feeble looking man could rise to such momentous occasions and inspire his men with such ardor as he did in the Shenandoah the year before.

The war of 1861 to 1865 was, I think apparent to all, a necessity.

Four millions of human beings were being held in bondage, and although the ordinance of 1787 had been passed by the Congress of the United States, and the British Commons had declared the slave trade *piracy* and would not consent to its further propagation, yet our country, notwithstanding, had permitted and continued to permit the landing of slaves at Pensacola, Florida, Charleston and Mobile, supply-

PROMINENT ANTI-SLAVERY MEN.

ing *Africans* to the great sugar and cotton plantations of the South.

It is not amazing or strange when a thoughtful mind reflects that there should occur some eventful scene among the nations of the world. How could a God of Justice, a God of Truth, sitting on his eternal throne allow what Wesley termed "an eternal lie" to longer endure?

It seems to me as though the ordained forces brought to bear were calculated and designed to strike a death blow to the impediments that marred the movements of the nations in their rise to progress to which they were destined to attain. The problem in the divinity which o'erclouds our ways was now revealed.

> No murky night, disguised by false alluring lights,
> No more shall e'er deceive them;
> A heaven-born truth in radiant light
> Is sent to mortal man to cheer him.

I had conducted my train a few days before to Five Forks, by order of the medical director, and at this time, I believe, I had my hospital corps organized and under perfect control, and I feel pleased today that it was so.

It had ever been my determination, should I succeed to the command, that I would so hold the power in my own hand that, come what may, the wounded should immediately be removed from the field, and any infraction of my orders should be punished then and there without the usual formality of a court-martial. It may not contribute to the popularity of this volume to say that I strictly adhered to this rule, but such is the case, and I dare not say I regret following such a course, the benefits arising from which are obvious, more especially when it is remembered that the care and responsibility of forty regiments were resting upon my shoulders.

Wilcox, our division commander, Hartranft, and scores of other brave men in the front holding their lives in their hands, having wives and children at home as dear to them as mine were to me, had full faith, should any accident happen to them, that they had a friend in the rear who would care for every want to the extreme limit placed under my control.

General O. B. Wilcox, who commanded our division through all these perilous scenes, when I first became acquainted with him, was to me the embodiment of an accomplished gentleman without that self-assurance and nonchalance found in a charlatan.

I never made but one request of him, which

was, that I make a detail for my own private convenience of a boy from the 8th Michigan. It was a rule with the General, in the conduct of his division, that all men fit for duty should carry a gun. I was cognizant of this when I asked him to grant me this favor. He hesitated a moment and then said: "Surgeon, you have been so faithful in the performance of your duty to my division that I cannot refuse you any reasonable request." The General was always extremely kind to me and recognized my services whenever he had the opportunity.

General Orlando B. Wilcox, the commander of the First Division, Ninth Army Corps, now lives retired in the city of Detroit.

When the soldiers' monument in the Campus Martius was dedicated to the brave men who enlisted from this State, ninety-five thousand strong, General Wilcox was elected to make the oration. No more beautiful language could have been employed than the General used on that occasion. The old First Division loved Wilcox and Wilcox loved them. In addressing them he said: "Men of the old First Division, we have suffered, endured and succeeded. Whatever our sacrifices may have been we have borne them without complaint. I welcome you here today as the remains of a valiant body of men who were determined, and I believe still are, cost what it might, to keep this flag that I now unfold in your presence floating over our heads." Governors, Senators, and all the municipal authorities of the city were present, but the most interesting personage was Major General Wilcox.

The 79th New York Highlanders, our old comrades, sent their delegation on this occasion, and Morrison, Laing and Moore, I remember, stood with bated breath and eyes filled with tears as the words fell from their General's lips.

It is utterly impossible for me to do justice here to many brave souls who were present that day, much less those who have passed away.

After the death, previously recorded, of Colonel Graves, Lieutenant-Colonel Ralph Ely assumed command of the old 8th.

Colonel Ely was a farmer previous to the war, residing at Alma, this State, He was a man of limited education as I understood, and yet had the inherent qualities of patriot and hero. Kind, indulgent and social with the men Ely, like Graves, would sacrifice life *ad libitum* in the performance of duty. Colonel Ely, it will be remembered, took command at the Wilderness and led them at every charge from Spottsylvania to Port Mahone, and with his little remnant, as the army advanced to Appomattox, guarded the railroad from Petersburg to Sunderland Station. Ely was inspired with an enthusiastic bravery that communicated itself to his men and made them forget self and know nothing but duty. He was twice elected Auditor General of the State since our return, and wore on his shoulders the star of Brigadier General. He died some years ago in the northern part of the State at a little hamlet named after himself. I do not remember a single incident where he was found lacking in any duty required of him. After receiving his brevet as Brigadier General in front of Petersburg, he was assigned commander of the second brigade of our old division, which he led into Petersburg on the evacuation of Lee. General Ely discharged his duties nobly and well, and was so endeared to us all that the boys gave him the sobriquet of "Papa" Ely.

The winter of 1864-5 was characterized by many serious and almost unaccountable results.

My field hospital was the depot into which was

gathered an immense amount of suffering, and yet, with the efficient aid that was rendered, all were made to feel somewhat comfortable. The constant movements by our flanks engaged the attention of us all, and we had become familiar with casualties of greater or lesser importance.

Beyond the Potomac, late in November, we continued to swing by the left to close in Lee's army.

The election was concluded, and the miasm which usually pervades at such times had cleared away.

General Grant determined, as we think today, to bring the rebellion to a crisis.

Sherman was advancing rapidly from the west to the sea.

An expedition was sent to shut up Wilmington, North Carolina, but the best devised methods made by military genius fail like others sometimes. Grant had resources within himself never before divulged. When Butler failed to carry Wilmington, he sent Terry who carried their works and opened up to the commerce of the Union that port.

It is rather amusing to think this result had not been obtained before. General Butler was, without doubt, a patriot, and served his country well, but he was a lawyer and lacked the military acumen which soldiers are supposed to possess. As I read the various accounts, written by those now deceased, I am forced to the conclusion that they, like others, had their differences of opinion.

Grant's fixed plan to secure Wilmington *must not* be thwarted. The army and navy, by his order, secured possession of those works, and Scofield, who, while under Thomas at Nashville broke up all Hood's lines, was transferred to the command.

No era in the history of nations—French, Austrian or Grecian—it would seem was fraught with greater events than were realized at that time. The great political question had been solved the November previous, "the rebellion must be subdued" was the verdict of the people, and every force was brought to bear to accomplish this result. Grant had been what many writers style an adventurer, but certain it is that success crowned his efforts.

Our wounded were sent to City Point, Virginia, where we occupied the depot after we crossed the James at Wilcox landing. The courtesies we here received I would like to notice at length, for certainly the patriotism shown by the women of the north should receive, late as it is, due recognition.

The operations of the army in front of Petersburg occupies a large part of American history of the rebellion, and although it may seem to my readers somewhat out of place to dwell at length on the various operations in which it was engaged, I think I may venture to say, without egotism, that no body of men secured grander results for their country than the First Division, Ninth Army Corps.

Field hospital, First Division, remained at the point stated, but when it was decided an advance should be made the medical director of the army ordered me to keep close up in their rear with an ambulance train and an efficient corps of stretcher bearers. It was about nine o'clock at night when I received his order, which I proceeded to obey.

We had, at this time, a good supply of surgical apparatus and all necessary equipments for a severe campaign. It was plain to be seen that heavy work was to be done. General Ely was occupying Petersburg in the place of Lee. Continuous heavy firing was in our front. Forts Hell and Damnation had been silenced, and not a sound from the drum corps or the band could be heard, which certainly seemed ominous to us at that time.

As we crossed the Weldon Railroad that night with forty ambulances, in command of Lieutenant Willey, the firing to our right and rear gave evidence that whatever failure the Army of the Potomac may have experienced heretofore, under McClellan or Grant himself, that death or victory could not now be long deferred.

We proceeded through the darkness of that night some fifteen miles, and encamped about four o'clock in the morning, when I directed the men to make coffee and eat their breakfast.

The Army of the Potomac must have occupied a line of twelve or fifteen miles, its right resting on the Appomattox as it flows into the James, its left covering all points east and south.

The "grip" was tightening closer and closer and it was easy to be discerned that we had reached a period in the history of the conflict which should be decisive.

It rained constantly from the time we left Petersburg until after we left Sunderland Station, and a more tired lot of men, mules and horses I never saw. My orders were peremptory: "Close up, as fast as possible," upon

Sheridan's cavalry and the Fifth Army Corps, which admitted of no delay. I remember well remarks made by Sherlock, Fitch and others of my staff, as well as wardmasters of the hospital, which seemed to convey the idea that I was overtaxing and asking more of them than human nature could well endure, but I could not take that into consideration at such a time. I paid little attention to their complaints, and as soon as our coffee was drank ordered an advance, for, from the firing in every direction, it was plain that deadly work was in progress on every side.

I was informed by the surgeon-in-chief, the day before, that I would be expected to care for all the wounded between Sunderland Station and Berksville on the Danville Railroad.

It is unnecessary to inform subordinates of all that is expected of them for the obvious reason if they are not appraised of all the dangers that beset them they are more easily controlled.

I conducted my train to the "Adams House," on the White Oak road, and there made my headquarters, and Sheridan rode up and down that road all that night and next morning, and if ever I heard profanity it was then. He had asked, on the 27th, that Wright's Sixth Corps might be sent to him, which from the way the troops were placed could not be given him, but was told he could have Warren's Fifth Corps.

Sheridan had peculiar notions of his own, and also a wonderful faculty of handling troops, he absolutely controlled the troops under his command and allowed no dictation from any quarter.

Phil. was a "raging lion" on the field of battle, and from a very intimate acquaintance with him I should judge there was but one of two motives paramount in his mind in the fifty or more battles he fought, and that was "death or victory."

I remember Surgeon Fitch, early in the morning, handing me a cup of coffee while sitting in the corner of a fence near the "Adams House," on the White Oak road, and laughing as Phil. cussed and d—d at Warren's tardiness in covering his rear. He had probably from eight to ten thousand cavalry at this time all exposed if Anderson or McLaws, or any other corps of Lee's army should strike him on his right flank, which he knew, should it happen, meant destruction to him.

Agreeable to Sheridan's ideas the right wing of Lee's army, swinging by their right, occupied works at Five Forks about midway between Petersburg and Berksville.

My hospital was still corraled at the "Adams House" under the command of Surgeon Roundy of the 37th Wisconsin Infantry. I went with his surgeon-in-chief to the front.

The surgeon-in-chief of the cavalry, Dr. G. McDonald, was always very courteous and requested me, if I had any desire, to accompany him on an inspection. He was a graduate of the University of New York—one of those astute, clear thinkers and fine operators in surgery which characterized but few of our army. He seemed to extend to me particular respect, undoubtedly arising from the care I had given the cavalry corps the night I had conducted them from Chancellorsville to Fredericksburg.

General Sheridan on that occasion seemed to me to be a most repulsive and contemptible brute. He did not notice or in any way return a salute, possibly this was because his mind was so pre-occupied with the battle which he knew must so soon occur. Two corps of the rebel army were crowding him. Custer, Merritt and Crook were now operating upon his flanks. A goodly number of wounded from Custer's Division were brought to the "Adams House," whom

I found, on my return, were well cared for by Dr. Roundy.

The night of the 31st was extremely dark, which did not permit of any operations at the front, but no time was lost at my field hospital in caring for and disposing of the wounded. Probably a more anxious night was never experienced by any army than that we endured, expecting either to hear of Warren's arrival or an attack at any moment, but neither Warren nor the enemy put in an appearance.

The next morning it seemed as though a terrible repulse awaited us, but the enemy was not anxious to hasten an engagement, until in the afternoon, when Sheridan's cavalry were dismounted and held the enemy in his works.

About three o'clock in the afternoon, on the 1st of April, 1865, it became apparent that the work in hand must be done, that either one or the other of the contending forces must be captured or annihilated.

I remember riding to the front to see the positions which the two forces occupied. I never shall forget how Phil. Sheridan, after waiting twenty long hours for Warren to come up, swore, and ripped, and tore. While he' was in such an excited condition Captain Comstock of his staff rode up to him and said, "General, two divisions of the Fifth Corps are right on hand," which cooled the General considerably and immediately changed the complexion of affairs.

The confused condition in which Sheridan's army was placed at this time was truly alarming.

It was expected of me to simply care for such wounded as were not provided for by the medical staff of the cavalry, and of course I shared the mutual anxiety of that night, being cognizant of the fact that we were disconnected from the main body of the army by four or five miles.

When Warren did arrive he seemed to be apathetic; did not put in his corps as General Sheridan desired and it certainly looked as though disaster must follow.

This dereliction of duty was reported to the Lieutenant-General who directed Sheridan to relieve him of his command, which Phil. was both ready and willing to do. When done, he wheeled Humphrey, Miles, Custer and Merritt into those terrible fastnesses at Five Forks and swept, as by a hurricane, all before him.

The battle of Five Forks was the first grand success won by the Army of the Potomac.

Very much credit is due to the cavalry arm of the service. Sheridan had established a fame that would live forever.

After Warren was relieved a new phase was developed in the art of war. Humphrey held the right, Murphy the left, and the cavalry, all *dismounted*, carried the position.

It was laughable to me as I witnessed the military audacity and acumen of Sheridan. No such manœuvre had been witnessed, to my knowledge, during the campaign, and it had often been remarked, by the infantry more especially, "who ever saw a dead cavalryman " (so imperfect had been the co-operation of their service), which, sanctioned by Grant, soon taught the Armies of the United States that rapid movements and "bull-dog grip" decide the issues of conflicts.

We gathered up of our men about one hundred and fifty wounded, which filled my train, who were immediately despatched to City Point in charge of Major W. C. Sherlock of the 51st Pennsylvania, Ninth Army Corps. The train immediately returned and overtook us at the junction of the Danville and Lynchburg railroads, where I was directed to establish a depot hospital.

CHAPTER VIII.

The victory obtained at Five Forks was pronounced, and had convinced Lee that Richmond could no longer be held, consequently couriers were despatched to the rebel government that an evacuation of their lines must be immediately undertaken. Jeff. Davis was in church when the message was handed him.

If any mortal man can question the authenticity or divinity of revelation which insures to the devil, and his minions a perfect recompense for the deeds done in the body we invite him to contemplate the scene now about to be enacted. Webster and Wilson of Massachusetts, Clay of Kentucky, Bingham of Michigan, and more than twenty other illustrious men had striven with him to convince him and his co-adjutors, who were intent on the destruction of the American Union, that a day of retribution would come.

The decree had gone forth from the God of all the earth and it was now to be executed.

There can be no question that there is (and

was in this matter) a divinity that shapes the end of nations as well as individuals.

Our brethren of the South had heretofore monopolized the government of this country. They had made our Congress, in all its legislation, contribute to the perfection of the acursed institution of slavery, and even gone so far as to pass what was known in its day as the fugitive law—compelling the people of the North to return to them any poor fugitive who might escape from their tyranny.

The decision made by Chief Justice Taney in the Supreme Court of the Nation upheld a band of conspirators who have today reached their retribution. In the trial of a slave he said a "*black* man has no right which a *white* man is bound to respect."

Christendom stands today aghast as she reads upon the pages of American law-givers such a dastardly and infamous decision. All the nations of Europe had ignored that doctrine, monarchial as they were. And it cannot be surprising to any reflective mind that God should visit such infamous jurisprudence with a terrible retribution.

Sheridan at Five Forks had, as was the custom at the cotton mills of Rhode Island, placed a *peg in the wheel*, which the watchmen in those days were required to do to show their employers they were attending to their duty.

In my study of military history I can not conceive of a more soldierly character than Philip Sheridan. Continuing his right half-wheel he closed in upon the column which escaped him at Five Forks, according to his own memoirs, from which I quote. He says:

"My cavalry pursued the enemy, driving Anderson's and skirting Lee's division, to a place known as the forks of the Deatonsfield road, forcing Gordon to abandon his line of march for Rice's Station, a point twenty-five or thirty miles beyond Berksville."

The confederate losses at the battle of Sailor's Creek was one thousand killed and wounded and six thousand prisoners.

There seemed to me, that afternoon, to have been wonderful sagacity exercised by that youthful cavalry commander, for he succeeded in securing the complete isolation of Ewell from Longstreet, driving Gordon well to his rear, and there is no doubt that if the main body of the army had seconded his efforts Lee must have been then and there annihilated. Here, as on many other occasions, there seemed to be a tardiness of movement on the part of the Army of the Potomac.

As the result proved, the battle of Sailor's Creek, way down in those pine woods of Virginia, was the decisive point which settled the great question of the American Rebellion.

It is true that the left wing of Lee's army yet possessed some vitality, but was so far depleted that it was plainly to be seen that it was in an exhausted condition which no vital force, inherently possessed by it, could ever resuscitate.

The battle of Sailor's Creek was one of the struggles between the contending forces whose importance seems to have been overlooked from the fact that other great events were transpiring at that time with the belligerent forces. The battle opened about 12:50 on the afternoon of the sixth of April, 1865. Sheridan had about eight thousand dismounted cavalry, every man with a six shooter and plenty of ammunition, and the Second and Sixth Corps of the Army of the Potomac, making the fire equal to about forty thousand Enfield rifles.

The rebels were mostly armed with Enfield rifles, and although they outnumbered us on this occasion, the rapidity of our firing was such as to more than overmatch them, so they were driven from the field, leaving a large number of prisoners and their dead and wounded in our hands. The wounded of both armies were soon collected, placed in ambulances and army wagons, and dispatched to Berksville, where field hospitals had been established. The Danville & City Point Railway which had been destroyed was now repaired and they were rapidly conveyed to rear hospitals.

'There had been heavy rains almost daily up to this time and the roads were almost impassable for loaded teams. From Sailor's Creek back to Petersburg the roads are rough at the dry season of the year, but now, where two armies like those of the North and South were continually passing over them, it can be easily imagined what their condition was at the worst season of the year.

The sufferings of the wounded from Sailor's Creek to Berksville were intense. After delivering our wounded at Berksville hospital the ambulances immediately returned and followed the operations of the army until the final surrender of Lee at Appomattox.

On the morning of the tenth of April we were ordered to return to Berksville and gather, on our way, all the wounded left at farm houses, as we advanced, which order was obeyed with alacrity.

On reaching Berksville we found the railroad thoroughly repaired, and the wounded were unloaded directly into the cars and sent to Northern hospitals.

Our hospital remained at Berksville until the morning of the 16th of April, 1865. The ambulance trains were busy in gathering in the wounded of both armies, this service being rendered not only to our own men but also to those who had heretofore been our enemies.

It was truly diverting to hear and answer the many questions asked by confederates now in the last ditch. One very prominent question often asked was: "What will *you'uns* do with *we'uns?*" and another: "*You'uns* are better than *we'uns* were made to believe."

The ambulance corps of all the division hospitals sought to treat our brave opponents with every kindness, and extended to them every comfort in their power; and it was amusing as we passed through the tents of that monster field hospital in which lay over one thousand wounded men, about equal numbers federal and confederate, telling their experiences in the great war through which they had recently passed, and see them smoke the pipe of peace. Surely the rebellion was not conceived by the masses of the south, but was the nefarious work of Cobb of Georgia, Davis of Mississippi, and their coadjutors.

About two o'clock of the afternoon of the 15th of April, 1865, General Meade, in special order, announced to the army the assassination of President Lincoln at Ford's theatre the night before. A copy of this order was left at the headquarters of our hospital.

The guard and attendants were ordered to form a line in front of our headquarters tent, and the order announcing one of the saddest events that ever occurred in the history of America was read. In rear of that line stood about one hundred confederates who had been slightly wounded and were being cared for by us. As our clerk read the order announcing the assassination of our beloved President a deep gloom seemed to settle upon all. I do not believe there was a dry eye in either line. I have no doubt if our boys had received the least encouragement they would have wreaked vengeance upon every confederate within their reach, and, so great was our fear of an outbreak, that a special order was immediately issued after the reading of General Meade's order, cautioning every member of our hospital against the commission of any overt act, which I am happy to say had the desired effect, quieting our boys and securing the safety and good treatment of the confederates in our charge.

The afternoon and evening of the 15th of April, 1865, will long be remembered by the attendants of the field hospital of the First Division of the Ninth Army Corps, whose duties were now almost terminated. A more devoted body of men I do not believe were to be found in the service than those who served under Dr. Bonine. They had discharged every duty up to December, 1864, with zeal and promptness. And I, as their surgeon-in-chief, take great pleasure in tendering those living my heartfelt thanks for the hearty co-operation I received from the surgeons, stewards, wardmasters, and nurses during the time I had charge of them.

On the morning of the 16th of April, our wounded having all left us, we struck the last hospital tent of the Army of the Potomac at Berksville, Va., and took up our line of march back to City Point, Va., where we went into camp and remained until the 23d.

During our stay at City Point, which was occasioned by lack of transportation, our time was mostly spent in visiting Richmond, Petersburg, Libby Prison, Belle Isle and other points of interest. The universal verdict of the people of both cities seemed to be that they were all heartily glad, both black and white, that the war was over.

On Wednesday, the 19th, the day of the martyred President's funeral, minute-guns were fired from all the military posts throughout the country. Several batteries were stationed at Petersburg, Richmond and City Point, all of which fired salutes throughout the day. It was truly a day of sadness and of mourning. I remember our Hospital Staff was unusually oppressed, being reminded, as they were by the sullen boom of those guns, of the departure of that brave soul. One thought filled every heart: "A great and good man, the father of his people, *had been murdered.*"

On the morning of the 23d of April a steamer arrived to convey us to Washington, D. C., where we disembarked on the morning of the 27th and marched through Washington, passing the White House, whose Corinthian columns were covered with black, as were all public buildings as well as numberless hotels and private houses, in mourning for the deceased President whose funeral train left on the 21st amid the silent grief of the thousands who had gathered to witness its departure.

It must have been a solemn sight as the dead President and the coffin of his little Willie were, by loving hands, tenderly placed in that funeral car and started for their western home, to be buried where his first struggles, trials and conquests were made.

We passed through Georgetown to near Tennallytown, where we were ordered to put up our tents and care for what sickness might occur in our division, which we found encamped a short distance from us.

We were lying here expecting every day to be mustered out and go to our homes, and naturally the men felt that the rules that were imperative during active service should be somewhat relaxed under existing circumstances. But day after day passed by and no order came to that effect, causing the men to grow so restless that it was necessary for the officers to be correspondingly vigilant to keep anything like discipline, for they would continually steal off to the city without a pass, which of course must, if not corrected, cause disorder. One man, I remember, had committed this offense several times, and was ordered to be tied up by the thumbs—a very unusual punishment—causing extreme pain. It was in this position that one of the medical staff found him, and, seeing the torture the man was enduring, cut the cords binding him, telling him to remain where he was until receiving further orders. Unfortunately this act was disapproved of by the commanding officer and greatly incensed him, but it was too late (seeing the war was over) to expect a continuance of strict military discipline; the time had passed for such extreme punishment.

Upon its becoming known that such extreme measures had been taken unusual indignation of line officers and men was manifested, but the whole feeling was quickly mollified by the man being ordered to his quarters.

At the beginning of June the regiment was ordered back into Washington, where they encamped to the right of the Jackson monument.

After our return to Washington many incidents like the foregoing occurred. Details were daily made to guard government property.

THE GREAT REBELLION.   199

The feeling of relaxation before referred to was naturally felt by officers as well as men, and on many occasions orders were violated by them which, while in front of an enemy, would have been strictly observed.

Our own Lieutenant Colonel seemed to have forgotten himself on many occasions, and indulged in practices which he would not have tolerated in any of his subordinates.

Washington at that day was full of all manner of men and women—especially women—whose enticing arts captured numbers of those who wore shoulder straps.

Private soldiers, who were in nowise fools, readily detected any deviation from the path of duty in their officers, and were eager to resent any orders which the officer himself ignored. A captain of the 8th Michigan Infantry, who had imposed very strict orders upon his men with regard to visiting saloons, became the worse for wear himself, one day, and came to his quarters somewhat over the "line." His men, perceiving this, were not slow to take advantage of his situation and quickly seizing him, bore him to the flag-pole, evidently intending to tie him up.

It happened that the surgeon-in-chief was the

only member of the field and staff present, and he, not wishing to see a fellow-officer disgraced, stepped up to the men and said: "Men, if you have any respect for your surgeon, please do not tie up the Captain."

Delos Warner (*a son of mischief*), of company B, shouted: "Hold on a minute, boys," and turning to him said: "Surgeon, don't you think it will do him good to tie him up a little while?" The answer was: "He is disgraced enough; take him to his tent and let him sleep it off." To their credit they did so, and within ten minutes two barrels of beer were rolled under the flag-pole as a compliment to the medical department.

CHAPTER IX.

The extreme restlessness which characterized all the troops about Washington during the summer of 1865 made the officers in command, and General Wilcox among the number, very anxious to have them mustered out of the service.

No Irish woman had a pig, no old Dutch woman a cow, all along Rocky Run, but received daily visits from our boys. What rations were not provided by our commissary were readily supplied by Delos Warner and other boys of the same stamp. It is my opinion they did not lack many of the comforts of life while we lay there.

Captain Hovey had charge of quite a number of Government buildings, and certainly understood the incomings and outgoings of soldiers, and yet, with all his watchfulness and care, he was utterly unable to stop the leakages which his guards (?) were set to protect. The soldiers had had many lessons in self-preservation during the war, and they had no idea of living on short rations while stationed at the seat of government.

The order of the day with them was "goodies," and our just regards.

It is fair to be presumed they would have been retained in Washington a much longer time but for the fact that they did not propose to guard property without possessing enough to make themselves happy.

This fact was soon apparent to the general commanding, and he ordered our muster out on the 25th of July, 1865.

CHAPTER X.

When the order to muster out was received the boys all collected around the flag pole, sent the Star Spangled Banner to its top, and united in singing that grand old anthem:

> "My country 'tis of thee,
> Sweet land of liberty,
>   Of thee I sing.
> Land of the pilgrims' pride,
> Land where our fathers died,
> From every mountain side
>   Let freedom ring."

My heart throbs today with the same feeling of patriotism as filled the bosom of our boys as they sang that song.

Four millions of human beings heretofore held as slaves, were now free. The national escutcheon was no longer "a living lie." The brightest anticipations of the Wesleys were realized; all men, of every race and color, stood, that beautiful July morning, equal before the law. The murderers of Lincoln had expiated their crime upon the gallows. The last expiring breath of the most stupendous conspiracy that history ever recorded had been wiped out of existence. Lincoln was in his grave at Springfield and Jeff. Davis was locked in Fortress Monroe. The mighty struggle between the brethren of the north and south was over, and the whole world stood in silence as the great republic arose from the ashes of the past and spread the flag that declared the freedom of this country and beckoned to the oppressed of all nations to share with her what had cost her so much—the boon of "life, liberty, and the pursuit of happiness."

On the morning of the 26th of July, 1865, we were marched to the depot and started homeward, reaching Pittsburg, Pa., the following morning, where the ladies had provided us a sumptuous breakfast. Then on to Cleveland, Ohio, where we found a splendid supper awaiting us, to which we paid ample tribute, and giving our benefactors three times three and a tiger, we continued our journey by steamer "City of Cleveland," arriving in Detroit early next morning.

The ladies of Detroit, we found, were not behind their sisters of other cities. They knew we were coming, and no millionaire of that commercial metropolis sat down to a better breakfast than was provided by the ladies of Detroit for the 8th Michigan Infantry.

Our old chaplain, George Taylor, whose health had been failing to such a degree that he had been compelled to resign, pronounced a beautiful invocation, after which, parting speeches were made by the surgeon of the regiment, and farewells were exchanged by that noble body of men, who had suffered and endured privations, gone hungry and almost naked, to sustain the constitution of their country.

The story of these men, many of them poor, some of them sick, and some holding the highest political and judicial offices in the State today, will be told by the coming generations of this beautiful Peninsular State.

A LEGACY.

A legacy we leave, not bought with gold,
  But with our blood is paid;
    Don't fail to hold with tightened grip,
Don't lose one star from off its fold.

CHAPTER XI.

The winter of 1864-65, and up to the time of our mustering out, was characterized by a great amount of suffering and sickness endured by our men, who had been through the war and had suffered all that falls to the lot of soldiers. Deprived of rations and half-clad fully one-half of the year, they had become physically impoverished to such an extent that their faces, from the rotund, had become gaunt and emaciated, and men of 25 years of age looked as though they were 40.

Having given in this work the names of the wounded, the same motive induces me to insert the names of the sick who were treated in the field hospital during the winter of 1864-65.

SICK IN FIELD HOSPITAL

Name.	Rank.	Co.	Regiment.	Disease.
Walker, H. B.	Pr.	A	20th Mich.	Diarrhea and typhoid fever
Pellett, Wm. B.	"	F	8th "	Diarrhea
Saxton, G. H.	Sergt.	B	1st Mich. S. S.	Varicocele
Minnis, Sam'l.	Pr.	F	20th Mich.	Chronic diarrhea
Horton, Wm. H.	"	"	8th "	Chronic diarrhea
Luikens, John	"	B	1st Mich. S. S.	Chronic diarrhea
Mendornoch, M.	"	E	27th Mich.	Phthisis pulmonalis
Hall, Geo.	"	I	2d "	
Brayman, Nelson	"	B	1st Mich. S. S.	Debility
Ready, Robert	"	"	" " "	Debility
Bair, Abraham	"	F	27th Mich.	Fever, intermittent
Archer, Andrew	"	K	2d "	Pneumonia
Ploss, A. B.	Cor.	"	8th "	Fever, intermittent
Cole, Warren	Pr.	A	" "	Old wound in hip
Tood, C. D.	1st Lt.	E	17th "	Rheumatism
Towns, Ichabod	Pr.	H	2d "	Pneumonia
Dimmick, Elmer	"	E	20th "	Epilepsy
Parish, Gilbert	Cor.	"	2d "	Old wound
Wolfram, Wm.	Sergt.	"	" "	Chronic diarrhea
Stockwell, Henry	Pr.	"	1st Mich. S. S.	Hemorrhoids
Robinson, H. F.	Lieut.	F	20th Mich.	Pleuritis
Brott, W. H.	Pr.	D	1st Mich. S. S.	Pneumonia
Smith, Uriah	"	I	27th Mich.	Anasarca
Prosser, T.	"	G	" "	Fever, remittent
Brown, A. M.	"	I	17th "	Phthisis pulmonalis
Pettengill, David	"	C	27th "	Jaundice
Melancanp, H.	"	B	20th "	Erysipelas
Chase, Uriah	"	2 s s	27th "	Diarrhea
Holmes, David	"	I	" "	Rheumatism
Davis, George	"	C	1st Mich. S. S.	Diarrhea

DURING WINTER OF 1864-5.

Admitted, 1864.	Returned to duty.	Sent to Gen. Hos.	Discharg'd	Furlough.	Died.	Remarks.
Nov. 1..					Nov. 9..	
" 1..				Nov. 2..		
" 1..				" 2..		
" 1..				" 2..		
" 1..				" 2..		
" 1..				" 2..		
" 1..				" 1..		
" 1..				" 1..		
" 1..				" 1..		
" 2..				" 2..		
" 2..		Nov. 5..				
" 2..		" 5..				
" 2..		" 5..				
" 2..					" 3..	
" 2..		Nov. 5..				
" 2..		" 5..				
" 2..					" 3..	
" 3..					" 4..	
" 3..					" 4..	
" 3..		Nov. 5..				
" 3..					" 6..	
" 3..		Nov. 5..				
" 5..		" 19..				
" 6..		" 13..				
" 6..			Nov. 11.			
" 8..		Nov. 19.				
" 10..	Nov. 13.					
" 11..		" 19.				
" 11..		" 19.				
" 11..		" 19.				

SICK IN FIELD HOSPITAL DURING

Name.	Rank.	Co.	Regiment.	Disease.
Hoyt, W. V.	Sergt.	D	17th Mich.	Incipient phthisis
Spaulding, G.	Pr.	B	" "	Idiocy
Leesott, J. B.	Cor.	C	" "	Opthalmia
Freeman, Geo. D.	Pr.	1 s s	27th "	Jaundice
Scott, Patrick	"	H	" "	Typhoid pneumonia
Warren, R. H.	"	F	2d "	Old wound
Green, Menhee	"	I	27th "	Congestion of lungs
Davis, Samuel	"	2 s s	" "	Pneumonia
Frany, Alfd.	"		" "	Hernia Inguinal
Porter, T. J.	"		" "	Ophthalmia
Folk, Andrew	"	I	" "	Anasarca
Chaffer, James	"	C	8th "	Jaundice
Elliott, John	"	K	" "	Rheumatism
*Kimball, Ch.	"	G	" "	Rheumatism
Nichols, F.	"	"	27th "	Fever, remittent
Wing, Wm.	"	I	" "	Fever, remittent
Elwood, Lyman	"	E	8th "	Diarrhea
Whisper, Isaac	"	C	" "	Erysipelas
Boyce, Michael	Sergt.	A	27th "	Fever, intermittent
Belland, Frank	Pr.	B	" "	Diarrhea
Finn, James	"	F	17th "	Whitlow, hand
Mills, Elihu	"	"	27th "	Debility
Switzer, A. M.	"	A	" "	Hemorrhoids
Davis, James	"	E	8th "	Diarrhea
Dimmick, Elmer	"	"	20th "	Epilepsy
Peck, J.	"	"	" "	Fever, remittent
Sanders, W. J.	"	I	" "	Debility
Morgan, M. S.	"	K	8th "	Fever, intermittent
Elliot, John	"	"	" "	Rheumatism
Durham, Alvin	"	F	" "	Chronic diarrhea

WINTER OF 1864-5.—*Continued*.

Admitted, 1864.	Returned to duty.	Sent to Gen. Hos.	Discharg'd	Furlough.	Died.	Remarks.
Nov. 11.	....	....	Nov. 11.			
" 11.	....	....	" 11.			
" 12.	Nov. 13.					
" 12.	....	Nov. 19.				
" 13.	....	" 19.				
" 14.	....	" 19.				
" 15.	....	" 19.				
" 15.	....	" 19.				
" 15.	....	" 19.				
" 15.	Nov. 26.					
" 15.	" 24.					
" 15.	" 18.					
" 15	" 18.					
" 15.	" 28.					
" 16.	" 24.					
" 16.	....	Nov. 19.				
" 17.	....	" 19.				
" 17.	....	" 19.				
" 18.	Nov. 28.					
" 18.	....	" 19.				
" 18.	....	" 19.				
" 22.	Nov. 28.					
" 22.	" 28.					
" 23.	....	" 26.				
" 24.	Nov. 28.					
" 24.	....	Dec. 1.				
" 24.	....	" 7..				
" 25.	....	" 1..				
" 25.	....	" 1..				
" 26.	....	" 1..				

SICK IN FIELD HOSPITAL DURING

Name.	Rank.	Co.	Regiment.	Disease.
McDowell, James..	Pr.	F	27th Mich.......	Gravel ....
Greening, John......	"	K	" "	Debility..................
Miller, A. F..........	"	"	" "	Fever, remittent ....
Paterson, J. Q........	1st Lt.	....	" "	Old wound................
Stockwell, H. M......	Pr.	E	1st Mich. S. S.	Chronic diarrhea.........
Billings, Milford....	"	C	8th Mich.......	Anasarca.................
Filkins, Alason.....	"	K	" "	Fever, intermittent.......
Porter, T. D..........	"	2 s s	27th "	Debility..................
McKellum, Neil....	"	I	17th "	Debility..................
Pearce, John	"	C	" "	Debility..................
Lounger, Peter......	"	E	" "	Debility..................
Mills, Thos..........	"	I	" "	Debility..................
Tounce, Lawrence..	"	"	" "	Debility..................
Hall, Frank	"	K	" "	Debility..................
Cole, Leonard......	"	G	20th "	Diarrhea.................
Holcomb, Julius ...	"	D	" "	Diarrhea.................
Thorn, J. Q. M.......	"	H	" "	Diarrhea.................
Prior, Earl..........	"	K	" "	Epilepsy ....
Isham, Owen A.....	"	"	2d "	Rheumatism..............
Farce, Henry L.....	"	D	27th "	Diarrhea.................
Dunn, Rich'd.......	"	"	2d "	Anchylosis...............
Babcock, Robt. A...	"	I	" "	Fever, intermittent......
Newton, A. C.......	"	B	8th "	Pneumonia...............
Hatch, Thos.	"	C	1st Mich. S. S.	Rheumatism..............
Calhoun, A. G.......	"	"	" " "	Rheumatism ....
Reed, James........	"	B	2d Mich.......	Debility ....
Davis, Randall	"	C	8th "	Rheumatism.............
Hicks, John	"	"	" "	Diarrhea.................
Seward, Wm. H.....	"	....	1st Mich. S. S.	Diarrhea.................
Kellogg, Chas.......	"	K	20th "	Erysipelas ....

WINTER OF 1864-5.—*Continued.*

Admitted, 1864.	Returned to duty.	Sent to Gen. Hos.	Discharg'd	Furlough.	Died.	Remarks.
Nov. 27.	....	Dec. 1..				
" 27.	....	" 1..				
" 27.	....	" 1..				
" 28.	Dec. 4..					
" 28.	....	" 1..				
" 28.	....	" 7..				
" 28.	....	" 7..				
" 29.	....	" 7..				
" 29.	Dec. 1..					
" 29.	....	" 6..				
" 29.	....	" 1..				
" 29.	Dec. 3..					
" 29.	" 1..					
" 29.	" 1..					
" 29.	....	" 7..				
" 29.	....	" 1..				
" 29.	Dec. 6..					
" 29.	....	" 7..				
" 29.	....	" 1..				
" 29.	Dec. 4..					
" 29.	....	" 6..				
" 29.	....	" 1..				
" 29.	Dec. 3..	....	1865. Mar. 3	....	....	Tuberculosis.
" 29.	....	" 6..				
" 29.	....	" 6..				
" 29.	....	" 6..				
" 29.	....	" 1..				
" 29.	....	" 1..				
Dec. 1.	....	" 1..				
" 1.	Dec. 3..					

SICK IN FIELD HOSPITAL DURING

Name.	Rank.	Co.	Regiment.	Disease.
Clymer, Isaac	Pr.	C	8th Mich.	Incised wound.
Gordon, G.	"	"	" "	Rheumatism.
Abbott, Ira	"	C	1st Mich. S. S.	Diarrhea.
Savery, C. H.	"	K	8th "	Fever, intermittent.
Cook, James	"	H	27th "	Diarrhea
Burns, W. H.	"	G	1st Mich. S. S.	Shell wound, right knee, fractured condyle, amputated lower 3d femur.
McColl, Tho. C.	"	B	" "	Shell wound, right leg, flesh
Kightlinger, Geo.	Cor.	F	8th "	Gunshot wound, head, fractured skull.
Kimball, Julius	Pr.	C	20th "	Diarrhea.
Ireland, Wm.	Pr.	D	1st Mich. S. S.	Diarrhea.
Bortel, John	"	B	20th "	Diarrhea.
Patterson, J. Q.	Lieut.		27th "	Gunshot wound, left arm and side
Heath, M. A.	Pr.	A	" "	Diarrhea.
Hathaway, Jas.	"		1st Mich. S. S.	Diarrhea.
Brewbacker, Sam.	"	C	8th "	Diarrhea.
Taylor, Henry	"	F	27th "	Contusion, hip.
Boyers, James	"	H	17th "	Contused wound.
Clark, T. I.	"	I	8th "	Lumbago.
Waddle, Tho.	"	E	27th "	Rheumatism.
Moore, Leander	"	H	8th "	Pneumonia.
Patrick, C. C.	"		17th "	Rheumatism.
Davidson, Curtis	"	A	1st Mich. S. S.	Rheumatism.
Knoll, John	"	G	" " "	Old wound.
McEwing, H.	"	D	2d "	Gunshot wound, head, right temple, destroying eyeball.
Hicks, Daniel	"	K	8th "	Chronic dysentery.
Susar, Moses	"	H	17th "	Diarrhea.
Robinson, A. F.	1st Lt.	E	20th "	Erysipelas.
Field, C. H.	Cor.	C	1st Mich. S. S.	Gunshot wound, head, slight
Houghtling, Hir.	Pr.	B	8th "	Gunshot wound, right arm, flesh
Morey, Edn. O.	"	H	2d "	Fever, congestion.

WINTER OF 1864-5 —*Continued.*

Admitted 1864.	Returned to duty.	Sent to Gen. Hos.	Discharg'd	Furlough.	Died.	Remarks.
Dec. 1		Dec. 1.				
" 2.	Dec. 7..					
" 3.	" 14.					
" 4.						
" 5.						
" 5.						{ Accidental explosion.
" 5.						} Accidental explosion.
" 5.						
" 6.	Dec. 7.					
" 7.						
" 7.						
" 7.		1865. Jan. 2..				
" 8.						
" 8.		-1864. Dec. 19.				
" 8.						
" 9.		" 17				
" 10.		" 19.				
" 10.						
" 10.		" 19				
" 10.		" 19.				
" 12.		" 19.				
" 12.		1865. Jan. 2				
" 12.	Dec. 16.					
" 13.		1864. Dec. 19				
" 13.		" 19				
" 13.		1865. Jan. 14.				
" 15.	Dec. 19.					
" 14.		1864. Dec. 19.				
" 15.		" 19.				Ball extracted.
" 16.		" 19.				

SICK IN FIELD HOSPITAL DURING

Name.	Rank.	Co.	Regiment.	Disease.
Swarthout, Theo...	Pr.	A	20th Mich........	Pneumonia...............
Lamb, Nelson......	"	I	8th "	Burn of face by powder..
Talbott, John.......	"	E	1st Mich. S. S.	Fever, intermittent......
Bell, Maurice.......	"	B	27th "	Gunshot wound, head, flesh...............
Rowe, J. H..........	"	G	8th "	Whitlow, hand...........
Bingham, S. L. J. S.	"	F	" "	Fever, intermittent......
Whetstone, W. H...	"	I S S	27th "	Diarrhea...............
Carpenter, T. S.....	Sergt.	E	20th "	Gunshot wound, right shoulder..... ....
Rodgers, A. A......	Pr.	I S S	27th "	Malarial, fever..... ......
Wright, Pettingill.	"	I	8th "	Inf., chron. pneumonia..
Waltz, Isaac........	"	G	27th "	Inflammation of eye......
Cooper, Gilbert.....	"	A	8th "	Dysentery ....
Gahegan, John	"	K	20th "	Abdomen, bullet penetrated.................
Cameron, Wm......	"	B	27th "	Chronic diarrhea.........
Patrick, C. C........	"	B	17th "	Rheumatism and general debility..........
Davis, Samuel......	"	A	1st Mich. S. S.	Rheumatism...............
Hall, Cornelius.....	"	K	" "	Diarrhea.................
Brophey, John C...	Lieut.	H	27th "	Rheumatism...............
Wright, Clark......	Pr.	I	1st Mich. S. S.	Pneumonia...............
Boyers, Ed..........	"	B	27th "	Mumps...................
Geller, Aug.........	"	I	20th "	Right foot, gunshot, flesh.................
Nichols, Francis....	"	B	27th "	Typhoid fever............
Hill, Wm............	"	K	8th "	Chronic rheumatism....
Renardin, C.........	Sergt.	G	1st Mich. S. S.	Intermittent fever........
Spotts, Rufus.......	Pr.	H	17th "	Continued fever ....
Dugnette, John.....	"	B	27th "	Typhoid fever............
Henman, Freeman.	"	H	8th "	Sprain...................
Williams, John.....	"	H	2d "	Right thigh, flesh wound.
O'Brien, John......	"	G	8th "	Pneumonia...............
Parkes, Asel........	"	D	27th "	Chronic diarrhea........

WINTER OF 1864-5.—Continued.

Admitted 1864.	Returned to duty.	Sent to Gen. Hos.	Discharg'd	Furlough.	Died.	Remarks.
Dec. 20.		1865. Jan. 2				
" 20.						
" 21.		Jan. 2.				
" 21.		" 2.				
" 22.	1865. Jan. 1.					
" 22.	" 13.					
" 23.		" 14.				
" 23.		" 2.				
" 24.		" 24.				
" 24.	Jan. 13.					
" 25.			Feb. 1.			
" 25.	Jan. 1.					
" 25.					Dec. 27.	Gunshot wound.
" 26.	1864. Dec. 27.					
" 26.			Jan. 14.			
" 26.		Jan. 2.				
" 26.	1865. Jan. 11.					
" 26.		" 2.				
" 27.		" 14.				
" 27.	1864 Dec. 30.					
" 27.		" 2.				
" 29.					1865. Jan. 15.	
" 30.		" 30.	" 2.			
" 30.		" 2.				
1865. Jan. 1.	1865. Jan. 20.					
" 2.					" 24.	
" 2.	" 30.					
" 3.		Jan. 14.				
" 4.		" 14.				Under arrest.
" 6.		" 14.				

SICK IN FIELD HOSPITAL DURING

Name.	Rank.	Co.	Regiment.	Disease.
Tubbs, Farley	Pr.	E	27th Mich.	Chronic diarrhea
Phelmo, David	"	D	" "	Rheumatism
Beland, Frank	"	B	" "	Asthma
O'Harra, Michael	"	G	" "	Bruise of chest
Smith, Uriah	"	I	" "	Remittent fever
Johnson, B.	"	G	" "	Deafness
Cooper, Gilbert	"	A	8th "	Chronic diarrhea and hernia
Mickel, Jeremiah	"	A	20th "	Shell wound, left arm, fractured ulna, Alacrenon process amp'td
Cook, Peter	Sergt.	K	27th "	Fever
Prior, E. W.	Pr.	K	20th "	Epilepsy
Ware, Stephen	"	C	8th "	Convulsions, typhoid pneumonia
Sayers, Jacob	"	F	20th "	Old wound, left leg, below knee
Jenne, Asa L.	"	G	2d "	Old wound
Kramer, Fred'k	"	D	8th "	Chronic rheumatism
Hammond, Tho.	"	B	20th "	
Gordon, G. S.	"	C	8th "	Diarrhea
Smith, G.	"	G	" "	Palpitation of heart
Brewer, J. H.	"	D	1st Mich. S. S.	Rheumatism
Nicholls, Henry	"	B	17th "	Anasarca
Hicks, Nelson	"	C	8th "	Remittent fever
Leeman, Wm.	"	F	" "	Bronchitis
Thomas, Joe	"	H	" "	Chronic diarrhea
Patterson, J.	"	B	" "	Diarrhea
Kiffer, John F.	"	B	" "	Bronchitis
Knowles, Seth	"	A	2d "	Gunshot wound, head, mortal
Eckerman, Alex.	"	D	8th "	Remittent fever
Huff, J. U.	"	K	27th "	Erysipelas
Brock, Wm.	Pr	I	8th Mich.	Diarrhea
Haywood, J. W.	"	K	20th "	Fever
Hammond, W. J.	"	B	8th "	Tumor

WINTER OF 1864-5 —Continued.

Admitted 1865.	Returned to duty.	Sent to Gen. Hos.	Discharg'd	Furlough.	Died.	Remarks.
Jan. 6.	Jan. 12.					
" 6.	....	Jan. 14.				
" 6.	....	....	....	....	....	On duty, hospital.
" 7.	....	Jan. 14.				
" 7.	Jan. 11.					
" 8.	" 28.					
" 9	" 15					
" 9.						
" 9.						
" 10.						
" 11.	....	....	....	....	Jan. 11.	
" 12.						
" 12.	Jan. 14.					
" 14.	....	Jan. 24.				
" 14.	....	Feb. 1.				
" 16.	" 20.					
" 17.	....	Jan. 24.				
" 18.	....	" 24				
" 18.	....	" 24.				
" 18.	....	" 24.				
" 18	Jan. 30					
" 18.	....	" 24.				
" 20.						
" 20.						
" 20.	....	....	....	....	" 22.	
" 22.	....	Feb. 1.				
" 24.						
Jan. 24.						
" 25.	....	" 1.				
" 25.	....	" 1.				

SICK IN FIELD HOSPITAL DURING

Name.	Rank.	Co.	Regiment.	Disease.
Hicks, John	Pr.	C	8th Mich.	Intermittent fever
McGee, John	"	D	" "	Chronic diarrhea
McCall, Barber	"	D	" "	Pneumonia
Howell, Henry	"	B	27th "	Bronchitis
McClellan, Ralph	Sergt.	B	1st Mich. S. S.	Pneumonia
Allen, Nathan	Pr.	B	" " "	Pneumonia
Filkins, Alanson	"	K	8th "	Malarial fever
Drost, Z.	Cor.	D	" "	Pneumonia
Weldon, Theon	"	B	2d "	Dropsy
Smith, Thomas	Pr.	E	27th "	Pneumonia
Smith, Jacob	"	I	20th "	Face and hands burnt with powder
Seymore, Joe	"	K	1st "	Left leg, contusion
Notz, Wm.	"	D	20th "	Varicose veins
Wildey, Geo. M.	Cor.	D	1st Mich. S. S.	Pneumonia
Jones, W. B.	Pr.	G	17th "	Intermittent fever
Oshan, Oren	"	K	2d "	Rheumatism
Needham, Joe	"	H	8th "	Anasarca
Cooper, G.	"	A	" "	Hernia
Grandy, M.	"	F	" "	Chronic bronchitis
Prast, Thomas	"	H	27th "	Diarrhea
Wilbert, Dolph	"	K	27th "	Scald
Hildreth, Oh.	"	C	8th "	General debility
Brott, Wm.	"	D	1st Mich. S. S.	Pneumonia
Carter, Amos	"	G	17th "	Pneumonia
Bush, Alex.	1st Lt.	B	20th "	Malarial fever
Hudson, Ed.	Sgt.Maj.		20th "	Left knee contused by shell
Morton, Bernard	Pr.	G	8th "	Debility
Fordham, Wm.	"	D	1st Mich. S. S.	Pneumonia
Stephens, Aug.	"	A	20th "	Gunshot wound, penetrated right lung
Allport, L. P.	"	A	8th "	Lumbago

THE GREAT REBELLION. 221

WINTER OF 1864-5.—*Continued*.

Admitted 1865.	Returned to duty.	Sent to Gen. Hos.	Discharg'd	Furlough.	Died.	Remarks.
Jan. 25.						
" 26.	----------	Feb. 10.				
" 26.						
" 26.	----------	" 10.				
" 27.	----------	" 1.				
" 27.	----------	" 1.				
" 27.	----------	" 1.				
" 28.	----------	" 1.				
" 31.	Feb. 14.					
" 31.						
" 31.	----------	" 1.				
" 31.	----------	" 1.				
Feb. 1.						
" 1.	Feb. 8.					
" 1.	Mar. 1.					
" 1.	----------	" 10.				
" 2.						
" 3.	Feb. 10.					
" 3.	----------	" 10.				
" 3.	----------	" 10.				
" 5.						
" 5.						
" 5.						
" 5.						
" 6.	Feb. 14.					
" 6.	" 11.					
" 8.	----------	" 10.				
" 9.						
" 9.	----------	----------	----------	----------	Feb. 11.	
" 9.						

SICK IN FIELD HOSPITAL DURING

Name.	Rank.	Co.	Regiment.	Disease.
Weaver, H.	Pr.	B	8th Mich.	Old wound, left arm
Barnum, T. M.	"	E	" "	Old wound, left foot
Graves, Morris	"	C	1st Mich. S. S.	Gunshot wound, left shoulder, flesh
Winters, Albert	"	G	8th "	Pneumonia
Roberts, Wm.	"	G	20th "	Rheumatism
Springer, Joe	"	H	27th "	Debility
Galleger, Dan	"	1SS	27th "	Rheumatism
Parminter, A.	"	G	20th "	Rheumatism
Sherman, J. A.	"	G	27th "	Rheumatism
Cooper, G.	"	A	8th "	Hernia
Wagoner, J.	"	F	" "	Old wound
Bonner, R. B.	"	F	" "	Paralyzed, left arm
Johnson, S. L.	"	C	2d "	Remittent fever
Brophy, J. C.	Lieut.	H	27th "	
Stocker, Irwin	Pr.	B	1st Mich. S. S.	Bruised hand
Ordway, I. J.	"	A	17th "	Kick by horse, right side.
Warncott, Peter	"	K	1st Mich. S. S.	Shell wound, fractur'd right femur
Young, Wm.	"	A	2d "	Incipient phthisis
Houston, J. H.	"	E	8th "	Scald foot
Richle, Martin	Sergt.	H	2d "	Left ankle contused, shell
Cartwright, Wm.	Pr.	F	" "	Right leg carried away, shell
Weston, Thomas	"	D	" "	Both thighs fractured by shell
Birmingham, J.	"	F	" "	Hand burnt with powder from unexploded shell
Hildreth, C.	"	E	8th "	Diarrhea
Westfall, J. H.	"	A	17th "	Inflammation of pleura
John, Wm.			1st Mich. S. S.	Abscess
Fry, Austin	Pr.	H	8th "	Lumbago
Armstrong, G.	"	G	" "	Gunshot wound, left nates penetrated
Connett, Isaac	"	H	1st Mich. S. S.	Pneumonia
Fields, Joe	"	I	27th "	Rheumatism

WINTER OF 1864-5.—Continued.

Admitted 1865.	Returned to duty.	Sent to Gen. Hos.	Discharg'd	Furlough.	Died.	Remarks.
Feb. 11.						
" 11.						
" 11.	....	Feb. 19.				
" 12.						
" 14.						
" 14.						
" 14.						
" 14.						
" 15.						
" 15.	Feb. 16.					
" 15.						
" 15.	" 16.					
" 16.						
" 17.						
" 18.	....	" 19.				
" 18.						
" 20.	....	....	....	....	Feb. 20.	
" 20.						
" 21.						
" 22.						
" 22.	....	....	....	....	" 22.	
" 22.						
" 23.						
" 24.	....	Mar. 1.				
" 24.	....	" 1.				
" 24.	....	" 1.				
" 26.	....	" 1.				
" 27.	....	" 1.				
Mar. 1.	....	" 1.				
" 1.	....	" 1.				

SICK IN FIELD HOSPITAL DURING

Name.	Rank.	Co.	Regiment.	Disease.
Twist, Thos. H.	Pr.	K	27th Mich.	Asthma and epilepsy.
McDonald, R.	"	D	" "	Bronchitis.
Kenewanebe, J.	"	H	1st Mich. S. S.	Pneumonia.
Pryor, Earl.	"	K	20th "	Pneumonia.
Smith, Henry	"	I	8th "	Burnt face by powder.
St. John, Chas.	"	K	27th "	Old wound and fractured ribs.
Miller, Nelson	"	1 s s	" "	Remittent fever.
Eldrich, L. W. H.	"	C	17th "	Fractured tibia.
Hatt, Henry E.	"	G	2d "	Pleurisy.
Pettingell, Da.	"	"	27th "	Remittent fever.
Lalond, Joe.	"	"	1st Mich. S. S.	Gunshot wound, third toe, right foot.
Smith, H. C.	"	I	" " "	Chronic diarrhea.
Young, Corne.	"	"	" " "	Rheumatism.
Bruce, W.	"	"	" " "	Debility.
Morris, G.	"	G	" " "	Intermittent fever.
Christian, H.	Lieut.	"	8th "	Bronchitis.
Filkins, A.	Pr.	K	" "	Jaundice.
Wagoner, J.	Corp.	F	" "	Old wound.
Doty, Don.	Pr.	B	" "	Old wound.
Black, John	"	"	" "	Chronic diarrhea.
Barnum, F.	"	E	" "	Old wound.
Hagar, John	"	C	" "	Intermittent fever, pneumonia.
Hill, W.	"	K	" "	Rheumatism.
Mether, A.	"	E	" "	Old wound.
Bonner, R.	"	I	" "	Paralysis.
Lash, H.	"	H	2d "	Intermittent fever.
Babcock, S.	"	"	" "	Intermittent fever.
Mead, A.	"	K	" "	Intermittent fever.
Parker, N.	Capt.	D	20th "	No diagnosis.
Moore, I.	Pr.	F	" "	No diagnosis.

WINTER OF 1864-5.—*Continued.*

Admitted 1865.	Returned to duty.	Sent to Gen. Hos.	Discharg'd	Furlough.	Died.	Remarks.
Mar. 1..		Mar. 1.				
" 1..		" 1.				
" 2..						
" 3..						
" 5..						
" 6..						
" 8	Mar. 9..					
" 9..						
" 11..						
" 12..						
" 13..						Amputated first joint.
" 14..						
" 14..						
" 14..						
" 14..						
" 14..						
" 14..						
" 14..						
" 14..						
" 14..						
" 14..						
" 14..						
" 14..						
" 14..						
" 14..						
" 14 .						
" 14..						
" 14..						
" 14..						
" 14..						

SICK IN FIELD HOSPITAL DURING

Names.	Rank.	Co.	Regiment.	Disease.
McDole	Pr.	F	20th Mich.	No diagnosis
Bissel, D.	"	G	" "	No diagnosis
Minnis	"	F	" "	No diagnosis
Sammons	"	I	" "	No diagnosis
Mash, Ch.	"	G	27th "	Nephitis
Johnson, R.	"	"	" "	Deafness
St. John, H.	"	A	" "	
McOhary	"	G	" "	
Kale, J.	"	B	" "	Sore leg
Kal, Jacob	"	H	" "	Old age
Crossman, T.	"	"	1st Mich. S. S.	Pneumonia
Haynes, J.	"	C	" " "	Chronic diarrhea
Febrelo, H.	"	E	17th "	Remittent fever
Heath, Milton, Prin. Musician.				Chronic rheumatism
Hett, John	Pr.	E	27th Mich.	General debility
Dingman, W.	"	A	1st Mich. S. S.	
Ireland, Thos.	"	D	" " "	
Thayer, A.	Bugler	G	" " "	
Miller, A.	Pr.	I	" " "	
Cassell, W.	"	"	" " "	Dropsy
Hawkins, J.	"	H	" " "	Rheumatism
Scott, A.	Sergt.	K	" " "	Debility
Robbins, E.	Pr.	A	" " "	Intermittent fever
Doyle, H.	"	"	" " "	Rheumatism
Deloney, J.	"	B	" " "	Old wound
Langland, J.	Cor.	B	" " "	Hernia
Eagle, Norman	Sergt.	"	" " "	Lameness
O'Brien, Tim.	Pr.	"	2d "	Gunshot wound, right hand
Peck, J.	"	"	1st Mich. S. S.	Gunshot wound, passing into cavity of abdomen
Agrison, Peter	"	K	2d "	Measles

THE GREAT REBELLION.

WINTER OF 1864-5.—Continued.

Admitted 1865.	Returned to duty.	Sent to Gen. Hos.	Discharg'd	Furlough.	Died.	Remarks.
Mar. 14..						
" 14..						
" 14..						
" 14..						
" 14..						
" 14..						
" 14..						
" 14..						
" 14..						
" 14..						
" 14..						
" 14..						
" 14..						
" 15..	....	Mar. 25.				
" 15..	Mar. 16.					
" 15..	" 16.					
" 15..	" 16.	" 25.				
" 15..	" 16.					
" 15..	....	" 23.				
" 15..	....	" 23.				
" 15..	....	" 23.				
" 15..	....	" 23.				
" 15..	....	" 23.				
....	....	" 23.				
....	....	" 23.				
....	Mar. 16.	" 23.				
....						
" 17..						
" 17..	....	....	....	....	....	Mar. 17.
" 18..	....	Mar. 25.				

SICK IN FIELD HOSPITAL DURING

Name.	Rank.	Co.	Regiment.	Disease.
McMullan, D.	Pr.	D	2d Mich.	Mumps.
Hardy, J.	"	G	8th "	Incised wound, left foot.
Nichols, H.	"	E	" "	Pneumonia.
Jaco, John	"	K	1st Mich. S. S.	Remittent fever.
Schlag, C.	"	H	20th "	Gunshot wound, back.
Circhey, W.	Cor.	C	2d "	Pneumonia.
Disbrow, J.	Pr.	B	1st Mich. S. S.	Pneumonia.
Hews, Sam.	"	H	2d "	Pleuritis.
Sanderson, W.	"	I	" "	Anasarca.
Lincoln, D.	"	F	20th "	Constipation.
McDonald, J.	"	G	8th "	
Easton, E. H.	"	F	" "	Convalescent but not able to fight.
Hildreth, C.	"	C	" "	
Kelly, Thos.	"	E	1st Mich. S. S.	Pneumonia.
Freer, Albert	"	H	" " "	Dislocated left shoulder.
Hampton, Wm.	"	C	8th " "	Hernia.

WINTER OF 1864-5.—Continued.

Admitted 1865.	Returned to duty.	Sent to Gen. Hos.	Discharg'd	Furlough.	Died.	Remarks.
Mar. 19..	....	Mar. 25.				
" 19..	....	" 25.	....	....	....	Cut with axe.
" 24..	....	" 26.				
" 24..	....	" 26.				
" 27..	....	" 27.				
" 31..	....	April 4.				
" 31..	....	" 4.				
April 1..	....	" 4.				
" 1..	....	" 4.				
" 2..	....	" 5.				
" 3..	....	" 5.				
" 3..	....	" 5.				
" 3..	....	" 5.				
" 9..	April 14					
" 19..						

CHAPTER XII.

For the gratification of many of my friends, and thinking it will be readily appreciated by those of my readers who are interested in the 8th Michigan Infantry, as well as being, possibly, the means of bringing into communication some old comrades of other regiments, I insert the names of *those living* of the 8th Michigan Infantry, thus, as far as possible, making my volume as complete and profitable, and, I trust, interesting, as the means in my power has enabled me to do.

The names and postoffice addresses of 8th Michigan Infantry, now living, are as follows:

ROSTER OF THE EIGHTH MICHIGAN INFANTRY.

Name.	Company.	Postoffice.	State.
Abram, John	B	Fowler	Mich.
Adams, Henry A.	A	Mt. Pleasant	"
Atherton, John J.	A	Bancroft	"
Austin, J. W.	B	Sheridan	"
Adams, John Q.	A	Flint	"
Austin, W. H.	G	Hazleton	"
Allen, Chas. D.	A	Montrose	"
Applebee, Hiram	G	Flint	"

SURVIVORS 8TH MICHIGAN INFANTRY.

Name.	Company.	Postoffice.	State.
Amos, J.	I	Owosso	Mich.
Allport, L. P.	A	Flint	"
Ackerman, John	I	Brigham	"
Andrews, O. G.	E	Dimondale	"
Bronson, A. W.	I	Bannister	Mich.
Benjamin, John B.	G	Fowlerville	"
Brooks, John Q.	B	Riley	"
Brown, Wm.	B	Bridgeville	"
Buckingham, L. G.	G	Detroit	"
Bell, Phares	C	Sumterville	Fla.
Bump, Orrin	A	Bay City	Mich.
Burbank, G. W.	A	Flint	"
Bowen, W. H.	H	Ann Arbor	"
Blood, Albert	E	De Witt	"
Beebe, Geo. C.	G	Bay City	"
Beckwith, F. L.	C	Fenton	"
Brooks, E. S.	C	Ithaca	"
Billings, Mulford	C	Fenton	"
Barnum, T. M.	E	Fenton	"
Brady, Samuel	C	Forestville	"
Buchanan, J. C.	D	Grand Rapids	"
Baker, Geo. P.		Detroit	"
Boucher, A. M.	A	Chesaning	"
Blaisdell, Dwight	A	Stockbridge	"
Biack, J. C.	B	Hastings	"
Brooks, Ransom	B	Lyons	"
Black, James H.	B	Sanborn	Dak.
Brown, Moses	B	Mt. Pleasant	Mich.
Barlow, Abner	C	Leslie	"

Name.	Company.	Postoffice.	State.
Beet, T.	D	Grand Haven	Mich.
Brott, Chas.	E	Hesperia	"
Bates, Austin D.	F	Marble	"
Bessmer, J. M.	F	Hastings	"
Blackenstore, J. H.	G	Advance	"
Brigham, Lafayette	G	Owosso	"
Bohn, J. H.	H	Oakland	Cal.
Brywater, Abe	H	Campbell	Mich.
Blinston, Thos.	I	Hastings	"
Britton, W. K.	K	Edgewood	"
Bedell, Allen B.	K	Menominee	"
Bedell, Aretus A.	K	Ypsilanti	"
Bliss, Oscar	B	Deerfield	"
Baldwin, Timothy	E	Shaftsburgh	"
Buckland, G. W.	C	Eaton Rapids	"
Bittner, Robert	I	Edgewood	"
Cheney, Alonzo	B	Mason	Mich.
Curtis, Albro	A	St. Johns	"
Canfield, W. S.	K	Ypsilanti	"
Cronk, Cyrenius	C	St. Louis	"
Clinton, A. D.	D	Ada	"
Chamberlin, A. H.	K	Detroit	"
Chapin, A. B.	D	Flint	"
Crowley, Bartholomew	D	Ionia	"
Cohoon, B. A.	K	Shepherd	"
Clymer, I. H.	C		
Carter, Mortimer	A	Flint	"
Clark, W. A.	H	Ann Arbor	"
Clayton, Thos.	K	Flint	"

Name.	Company.	Postoffice.	State.
Card, Oscar F.	I	Corunna	Mich.
Callin, Levi H.	A	Grand Blanc	"
Clemens, Willard	F	Richfield	"
Clothier, Harlon	A	Flint	"
Curtis, G.	A	St. Johns	"
Crapser, C. A.	A	Swartz Creek	"
Cottrell, A.		Lansing	"
Clifford, W. H.	B	Austin	Nev.
Campbell, Austin	C	Salt River	Mich.
Childs, Philander	C	Salt River	"
Clark, William	C	Alma	"
Crowley, Patrick	C	Ionia	"
Church, Matthew	C	Ithaca	"
Clark, Isaac	E	Coral	"
Chadwick, Henry	E	Coe	"
Cock, Chas. F.	F	Hastings	"
Cole, Emmett	F	Columbia	Dak.
Cole, Harlan	F	Tustin	Mich.
Cannon, Wm.	G	Tecumseh	"
Coleman, Wm.	G	Dentons	"
Colyer, W. R.	H	Hart	"
Camus, P. F.	I	Lowell	"
Curtis, John	K	Fitchburg	"
Call, Henry C.	K	Bancroft	"
Chandler, Geo. W.	A	Detroit	"
Cartwright, Chas.	A	Flint	"
Campton, Alonzo	I	Freeland	"
Caldwell, H. W.	A	Pulaski	N. Y.
Challee, James	E	Jackson	Mich.
Close, Wm. F.	F	Byron	"

Name.	Company.	Postoffice.	State.
Carey, H. E.	A	Weimar	Texas.
Clark, T. F.	I	Corunna	Mich.
Dougherty, John	B	Lyons	Mich.
Dibble, Clark	G	Fenton	"
Dennis, E. H.	K	Jackson	"
Dickerson, W. F.	F	Grand Rapids	"
Dooling, Jerry	B	St. Johns	"
Decker, Louis	I	Carlton Center	"
Dean, Chas. H.	D	Grand Rapids	"
Dye, Chas.	A	Flint	"
Denton, Emery	A	Grand Blanc	"
Dickerson, Erastus	K	Flint	"
Dart, Edward	G	Swartz Creek	"
Doyle, H. R.		Martinez	Cal.
Donahue, James		South Haven	Mich.
Darling, Ben.	K	Jackson	"
Douglas, Geo.	B	Elm Hall	"
Doty, Alonzo	B	Bridgeville	"
Drew, Fred.	B	St. Johns	"
Davis, Rudolf	C	Cross Village	"
Dalzelle, John A	D	Muir	"
DeMond, Wm.	F	Augusta	"
Dowd, John	F	Hickory Corners	"
Darling, Diadamus	G	Holton	"
Deer, John	G	St. Clair	"
Derts, A.	H	Hesperia	"
Downey, John J.	K	Detroit	"
Dickson, Anson	Band	Blissfield	"
Doane, J. W.		Forest Hill	"

Name.	Company.	Postoffice.	State.
Drury, Geo. D.	A	Tecumseh	Mich.
Davidson, John	E	Lansing	"
Dye, Oliver	K	Flushing	"
Disness, Chas.	I	Corunna	"
Eggleston, C. J.	A	Flint	Mich.
Elwood, L. W.	E	Dimondale	"
Eckman, John W.	I	Bingham	"
Eddy, B. D	A	Fenton	"
Eggleston, Chas. B.	K	McBride	"
Edger, Thos.	B	Ionia	"
Eastmon, Alonzo	C	Alma	"
Eckerman, A. H. H.	D	Muskegon	"
Elkins, J.	E	Grand Ledge	"
Ellis, Carlton	Band	Blissfield	"
Frankland, E.	B	North Star	Mich.
Foster, L. S.	I	Gaines	"
Fisher, Elijah H.	H	Grand Rapids	"
Face, Marcus	B	Maple Rapids	"
Flint, Horatio	G	Davison	"
Fuller, D. K.	E	Lansing	"
Freeman, Chas.	I	Owosso	"
Fox, Wells B.	Surg.	Bancroft	"
Frost, David	B	Ashley	"
Fuller, Geo. B.	K	Clyde	Ohio.
Foote, Geo. W.	G	Flint	Mich.
Fenton, J. Brush	G	Flint	"
Feister, W.	C	Alma	"
Flower, E. W.	E	Bay City	"
Fuller, Geo.	G	Flushing	"

Name.	Company.	Postoffice.	State.
Finch, Lorenzo	K	Hanover	Mich.
Gleason, Frank	B	Lyons	Mich.
Greenfield, O. H.	F	Hastings	"
Goodman, D. K.	H	Greenville	"
Grubaugh, Jacob	B	Bridgeville	"
Green, Jonathan	H	Saranac	"
Guilmore, Samuel	H	Greenville	"
Gillis, Andrew	A	Flint	"
Green, Ira	A	Lapeer	"
Green, Oscar	H	Jackson	"
Graves, H. M.	D	Detroit	"
Gavett, W. A.	E	Grand Rapids	"
Galligan, Michael	F	Grand Rapids	"
Guntrip, Abram	F	Nashville	"
Grebel, Henry	F	Grand Rapids	"
Ganson, Theodore	G	Mesaville	A. T.
Gilbert, E. N.	H	Ann Arbor	Mich.
Gibson, John	G	Flint	"
Hart, H. S.	C	St. Johns	Mich.
Hamilton, W. E.	G	St. Johns	"
Holmes, Walter	G	Salem	"
Hammond, Jay	B	Fowler	"
Hines, H. W.	F	Edmore	"
Holmes, Eugene R.	B	Owosso	"
Hildreth, Chas.	C	Alma	"
Halsted, Wallace	B	Lyons	"
House, H. W.	I	Stanton	"
Hendee, O. P.	I	Collins	"
Hunt, C. N.	B	Brice	"

Name.	Company.	Postoffice.	State.
Herrington, A. J.	C	St. Louis	Mich.
Hubbs, Charles	E	Greenville	"
Hildreth, W. J.	B	Detroit	"
Hagar, John	C	Caro	Mich.
Hill, Alva	E	Deer Lake	"
Hickman, Clement	C	Red Bluff	Cal.
House, John	C	Alma	Mich.
Hovey, E. M.	C	Fenton	"
Harding, A. L.	A	Tawas City	"
Hicks, John	F	Flint	"
Hamp, N. B	C	Elm Hall	"
Hews, Henry M.	F	Edmore	"
Holden, Wm.	F	Bedford	"
Hollinbury, Geo.	I	Dundee	"
Hale, P. M.	K	Eaton Rapids	"
Hill, John	K	Flint	"
Harrington, Geo. L.	E	Sandstone	"
Hull, Geo.	B	Carson City	"
Ioegalls, Ira	G	Flint	Mich.
Jewell, Wm.	G	Flint	Mich.
Judd, Wm.	E	Lake View	"
Johnston, Wm.	K	Bunker Hill	"
Jewell, Geo. W.	I	Vernon	"
Jennings, A. B.	A	Swartz Creek	"
Jewett, L. E.	B	Aurelius	"
Judd, Wm.	C	Saginaw	"
Jewett, Samuel	F	Hazelton	Dak.
Joslin, Wm.	K	Forestville	Mich.
Johnson, John Q. A.	C	Mt. Pleasant	"

Name.	Company.	Postoffice.	State.
Jackson, J. F.	K	Jackson	Mich.
Kinley, E. H.	C	Alma	Mich.
Kriss, G. E.	C	Alma	"
Kibbee, Elijah A.	F	Okemos	"
King, R. R.	A	Albion	"
Kimball, Enos	C	Alma	"
Kinsman, W. E.	E	Sparta	"
Kurrie, Fred	F	Wilmington	Cal.
Longyear, W. D.	C	Mason	Mich.
Loveland, Samuel	C	Alma	"
Leeland, Wm. M.	A	St. Johns	"
Lane, Isaac C.	C	Elba	"
Long, C. D.	A	Flint	"
Lewis, Fletcher	A	Denver	Col.
Loomis, Monroe	C	Salt River	Mich.
Leeman, Wm.	F	Sebewa	"
Love, Geo. W.	I	Grayling	"
Longstreet, Wm.	E	Lansing	"
Lewis, John D.	G	Carlton Center	"
Mersthen, E. A.	E	Howell	Mich.
Marsh, B. F.	G	Fenton	"
Mosher, D. H.	B	Pewamo	"
Myers, Nicholas	K	Oak Grove	"
McWain, J. B.	F	Big Rapids	"
Moore, H. N.	D	Grand Rapids	"
Maloney, Thos.	K	Jackson	"
Miller, Chas. E.	K	Jackson	"
McLaughlin, S.	C	Detroit	"

THE GREAT REBELLION.

Name.	Company.	Postoffice.	State.
Marsh, E. C.	H	Flint	Mich.
Miller, Fred	B	Fowler	"
Montoyne, Robert	D	Flint	"
McComas, D. H.	E	Lansing	"
Mathews, Lafayette.	G	Gagetown	"
McWilliams, Orville		Flint	"
Montgomery, H. J.	C	Davisburg	"
McCumber, F. W.	C	Fenton	"
Miner, Wm. P.	K	Hillsdale	"
McNitt, O. B.	G	Flint	"
McCrery, Chas.	H	Chetopa	Kan.
Maus, Jacob		Hastings	Mich.
Mitchell, James H.	A	Leslie	"
Maxted, Chas.	B	Elwell	"
Mansfield, M. M.	B	Hesperia	"
Murdock, Chas.	B	Fowlerville	"
McClellen, G. S.	E	Gowan	"
McCarty, Thos.	E	Lapeer	"
Matthews, A.	E	Mt. Clemens	"
McClellan, G.	E	Greenville	"
Merrifield, Isaac	F	Columbia	Dak.
Maile, John S.	F	Denver	Col.
Michael, John	F	Hastings	Mich.
McKenzie, Daniel	F	White Hall	"
Mead, James F.	F	Hastings	"
McBain, Duncan	F	Hickory Corners	"
Mason, George	F	Big Rapids	"
Marvin, Chas.	G	McBride	"
Mills, James	H	Mancelona	"
Morgan, Geo. W.	K	Leslie	"

Name.	Company.	Postoffice.	State.
Monger, Seth	K	Freeland	Mich.
Monger, Miles	H	Freeland	"
McGraw, Chester	K	Jackson	"
Morse, Hewlett F.	E	Grand Rapids	"
Martin, W. R.	A	Jackson	"
Newell, Geo. E.	A	Flint	Mich.
Newton, A. C.	B	Lowell	"
Nye, Wm.	F	Kalamazoo	"
Newton, Augustus	F	Hastings	"
Noah, J. H.	H	Stanton	"
Noble, Wm.	K	Fremont	"
Nelson, Wilbur	C	Ithaca	"
Owen, John	G	Fenton	"
Odell, Myron	A	Mundy	"
Overton, A. V.	G	Morenci	"
Pecktil, Darius	B	Ashley	Mich.
Phelps, John P.	F	Hastings	"
Patterson, J. L.	B	Maple Ridge	"
Pulver, H. H.	E	Laingsburg	"
Pratt, W. R.	A	Flint	"
Parker, Wm.	G	Clio	"
Persons, James H.	A	Elk	"
Palmer, Wm.	G	Fenton	"
Phillips, Jacob	G	Flint	"
Pelton, L.	E	Jackson	"
Phillips, Travis	F	Hastings	"
Pier, Henry	C	Ely	"
Palmer, Chase B.	F	Nashville	"

THE GREAT REBELLION. 241

Name.	Company.	Postoffice.	State.
Pierce, Daniel	F	Cedar Creek	Mich.
Perry, James S.	F	Nashville	"
Pratt, Geo. B.	F	Argentine	"
Powers, Wm. H.	F	Hastings	"
Potter, Geo.	H	Chase	"
Patchen, Anson	K	Grass Lake	"
Phillips, Mark	K	Rives Junction	"
Pellett, W. B.	F	Flint	"
Predmore, J. E.	K	Orion	"
Parker, D. C.	A	Reed City	"
Pratt, Delos	A	East Jordan	"
Rossman, Harman	H	Lake View	Mich.
Reese, James	B	Fowlerville	"
Rooks, Charlie	C	St. Louis	"
Ranger, Thos. H.	B	Lyons	"
Roe, J. H.	G	Flushing	"
Reamington, L. A.	A	Swartz Creek	"
Robinson, B.	K	Flint	"
Rowley, Joseph	C	St. Louis	"
Richter, C.	D	Hart	"
Runyan, Chas. M.	F	Grand Rapids	"
Roush, John	F	Miller Station	"
Ransom, Geo. H.	K	Jackson	"
Rosecrans, Jackson	E	Carson City	"
Rouse, John	F	Mettles	"
Striker, Edward	K	Harrison	Mich.
Shumway, Wm.	K	Jackson	"
Spears, Henry	K	New Buffalo	"
Stevens, James A.	K	Muskegon	"

Name.	Company.	Postoffice.	State.
Stowell, Samuel	B	Ionia	Mich.
Strayer, Michael	C	Elm Hall	"
Strayer, H. K.	C	Elm Hall	"
Sage, Wm.	B	Fowler	"
Snell, W. H.	B	Oak Grove	"
Shattuck, E. S.	A	Ionia	"
Schwartz, Fred	B	Fowler	"
Smith, Thos.	B	Ionia	"
Spears, High	I	Vernon	"
Sears, Jacob	B	Pewamo	"
Sawyer, B. F.	G	East Saginaw	"
Spencer, Harvey	F	Hastings	"
Snyland, Hiram	A	Edmore	"
Smith, W. H.	B	Greenbush	"
Spaulding, D. C.	G	Detroit	"
Smith, W. R.	I	Owosso	"
Seaver, Wm. E.	B	Pewamo	"
Salnave, T. H.	H	Saginaw	"
Shattler, Anthony	I	Kenoukee	"
Swinsco, Geo. E.	I	Chicago	Ill.
Swart, Stephen	A	West Bay City	Mich.
Sumner, John D.	D	Kalamazoo	"
Smith, A. J.	B	Ludington	"
Seaver, Wm. E.	B	Ludington	"
Sears, Jacob	B	Clare	"
Strong, J. A.	D	Grand Haven	"
Sayers, Wm.	D	Holton	"
Spencer, Chas. D.	E	Greenville	"
Swartout, Chas.	F	Cross Village	"
Sixbury, Benj.	F	Ashland	"

THE GREAT REBELLION. 243

Name.	Company.	Postoffice.	State.
Sipps, Benj.	F	Ravenna	Mich
Seeley, Hiram	F	White Cloud	"
Snyder, Chas.	F	South Bend	Ind.
Simmons, Addison	K	Jackson	Mich.
Sullers, Andrew J.	C	Flint	"
Sureto, John	E	Lansing	"
Shipp, Fred	E	Lansing	"
Tirrell, Chas.	E	Webberville	Mich.
Tracy, Will	K	Flint	"
Turner, Geo. H.	A	Flint	"
Todd, H. E.	A	Flint	"
Taylor, Frank	D	Mundy	"
Terwilager, H.	B	Carson City	"
Tallman, H. V.	C	Mason	"
Thomas, M.	G	Grand Haven	"
Taylor, Rev. Geo.	Chap.	Detroit	"
Vanderveen, A.		Grand Haven	Mich.
Verhock, G.	D	Grand Haven	"
Van Ness, Richard	H	Greenville	"
Walker, Moses	A	Goodrich	Mich.
Wheeler, Washington C.	H	Dansville	"
Wright, John S.		Riverdale	"
Wing, C. A.	G	Howell	"
White, Eugene	C	Shepherd	"
Winter, S. J.	H	Grand Ledge	"
Wing, Warren	H	Dashville	"
Walker, Chester	C	Alma	"
William, Geo.	F	Nashville	"
Wills, Geo. A.	A	St. Johns	"

Name.	Company.	Postoffice.	State.
Wilson, J. C.	Surg.	Flint	Mich.
Waganer, John	F	Elkhart	Ind.
Wheeler, Wm. A.	G	Flint	Mich.
Willett, Ed.	B	Bridgeville	"
Willey, M. L.	H	Atlanta	Ga.
Whitmore, F.	I	Duffield	Mich.
Wooster, S. R.	Surg.	Grand Rapids	"
Williams, H. H.		Fentonville	"
Wells, Chas. A.	A	McBride	"
Warner, John A.	A	Millington	"
Wetherbee, Amos	B	Eureka	"
Wait, D. M.	C	Burr Oak	"
Wolf, Israel	C	Alma	"
Wolf, Solomon	B	Salt River	"
Wilbur, Henry	E	Webberville	"
Wheeler, W. R.	F	Hastings	"
Warren, Stanley	F	Lacey	"
Warren, J. B.	F	Alpena	"
Whitney, E.	F	Clare	"
Whitney, M. E.	F	Clare	"
Woodbury, Wm.	G	Mt. Pleasant	"
Wilkinson, Geo.	G	Gilford	"
Winter, D. J.	H	Soldiers' Home	"
Welch, Henry K.	K	Mt. Pleasant	"
Warner, Lossen S.	B	Cavour	Dak.
Webster, Lewis	A	Flint	Mich.
Wiley, A. M.	C	Alma	"
Washburn, Asahel C.	E	South Lyon	"
Woodman, J. S.	G	Prairieville	"
Young, Eugene	I	Owosso	Mich.
Zimmerman, John	C	Sheridan	Mich.

CHAPTER XIII.

The following are the names of the commissioned officers who were mustered out of the service, July 30, 1865:

CAPTAINS.

Charles H. Swartout, July 30, 1865, with regiment.
James P. Dodge.
Henry J. Christian.
John A. Elder.
Charles H. McCreery, October 7, 1865.
Samuel A. Baldwin.
Edwin Hovey.
Martin L. Wiley.
Edward R. Chase.
Daniel L. Holway.
J. Edward Marum, November 9, 1864, expiration of term.
G. B. Fuller, January 8, 1865.

FIRST LIEUTENANTS.

William Tracy.
Charles G. Watkins.

Bartley Siegel.
Timothy L. Baldwin.
Benjamin F. Pease.
Simeon McLaughlin.
Andrew H. Gillies.
John R. Dougherty.
Oscar P. Hendee.
Harrison H. Williams, November 17, 1864,. for disability.
— Phillips, 1864, expiration of term.
Baker, George P., Quartermaster.
Doane, J. W.
Bump, Orrin.
Chase, Edward B.
Clifford, William.

SECOND LIEUTENANTS.

Harman Roseman.
Charles H. Snyder.
James Cooper.
James Meade.
John Williams.
Nathaniel K. Haynes.
George C. Beebe.
Townsend A. Ely.
Henry Clark.
Joseph B. Fenton.

HOSPITAL STEWARDS.

Melton M. Fenner, 1861.
Arend Vanderveen, to 1863.
Thos. Eagleston, to 1S64.
John Michaels, 1864 (August and September).
Colonel D. Johnson, 1862.
Alexander Ackerman, 1864 (September and November).
Myron G. Southwick, 1864-5 (December to July, 1865).

Captains George E. Swinscoe, formerly Captain of Company I, — Smith, of Company C, J. Edward Marum and George B. Fuller, were all accomplished gentlemen and thorough soldiers, whose time having expired, were mustered out in 1863.

With but few exceptions the commissioned officers who were mustered out with the regiment had obtained their present rank by virtue of their soldierly qualities and general conduct, and we question whether any class of men were more deserving of honor than those who rose from the ranks.

Of these, the majority took with them, when they left the service of their country, mementoes of their fidelity and bravery in the conspicuous absence of various members of their body and ugly scars which they received in the discharge of their duties, some of whom deserve especial mention.

Captain James S. Donahue was twice severely wounded. Once at James Island, where his right shoulder blade was destroyed, and again at the Wilderness, where he lost his left thigh, which effectually closed his fighting career; but he was remembered by many long after for his goodness of heart combined with many excellent traits of character.

Captains John A. Elder, Edwin M. Hovey, and Daniel L. Holloway also bear upon their persons ugly marks which were received from rebel bullets while defending the flag of their country.

First Lieutenants Charles G. Watkins, Timothy L. Baldwin, Andrew H. Gillies, John R. Dougherty, Oscar P. Hendee and Lewis Webster (who fell terribly wounded in front of Petersburg as he bore the flag in front of his regiment) are men deserving of the admiration of their countrymen for the pluck and bravery shown in their various engagements.

Of Second Lieutenants who wear badges of honor in the shape of great scars, made by bullet and shell in the thick of the fight, we mention : Harman Roseman, Charles H. Snyder, James Cooper and James F. Meade, the last named carrying today a minie ball in his lungs from the time of the explosion of the mine in front of Petersburg, July 30, 1864.

Major George W. Chandler, now of Detroit, was one of the first to enlist at the formation of the regiment, as sergeant of Company E. By reason of his marked business ability promoted, April 13, 1862, as Second Lieutenant, and made Division Commissary ; commissioned First Lieutenant Company A, September 1, 1862, and made Post Commander at Belle Plains, Va., in February, 1863; promoted as Captain and Commissary of Subsistence United States Volunteers, May 8, 1864; breveted Major, for faithful service in that department, at the close of the war.

First Lieutenant George Wells, of Company C, acted as Commissary of First Brigade, First Division, Ninth Army Corps, and was honorably discharged as such July 30, 1865.

The following is a list of surgeons and assistant surgeons of the regiments and their places of residence whose wounded are herein recorded :*

1st Michigan Sharpshooters.

Surgeon Arvin F. Whelan, Hillsdale, Mich., from January, 1863.

ASSISTANT SURGEONS.

Jacob B. McNett, Grand Haven, Mich, to April, 1864.

Asahel B. Strong, Reading, Mich., to July, 1864.

Thomas Eagleston, Parkersburgh, Ill., from August, 1864.

George F. Cornell, St Clair, Mich., to December, 1863.

Doctor Whelan of this regiment rendered valuable service at the Field Hospital, First Division, Ninth Army Corps, and was a prominent member of its operating staff.—*Now deceased.*

2d Michigan Infantry.

SURGEONS.

Alonzo B. Palmer, Ann Arbor, to September, 1861.

Evan J. Bonine, Niles, Mich., to September, 1864.

Samuel M. Holton, from April, 1865.

ASSISTANT SURGEONS.

H. A. Clellan, Detroit, Mich., to April, 1864.

H. F. Lyster, Detroit, Mich., to July, 1862.
J. Robbins, Hubbardston, Mich., from April, 1865.
R. S. Vickery, United States Army, to March, 1865.

8th Michigan Infantry.

SURGEONS.

Hulbert B. Shank, Lansing, Mich., to January, 1862.
James C. Wilson, Flint, Mich., to March, 1863.
Wells B. Fox, Bancroft, Mich., from July, 1863.

ASSISTANT SURGEONS.

Samuel R. Wooster, Grand Rapids, Mich., to April, 1863.
John Willett, Flint, Mich, to December, 1864.
A. Vanderveen, Grand Haven, Mich., from June, 1863.

17th Michigan Infantry.

SURGEONS.

A. R. Calkins, Allegan, Mich., to October, 1862.
J. D. Bevier, from October, 1862.

ASSISTANT SURGEONS.

A. H. Daniels, Galesburg, Mich., from October, 1862.

Delos L. Heath, to July, 1863.

L. H. Cooper, Monroe, Mich., to October, 1864.

F. R. Crosby, Napoleon, Mich., to April, 1864.

20th Michigan Infantry.

SURGEONS.

Simeon S. French, Battle Creek, to July, 1864.

Orville P. Chubb, Omaha, Nebraska, from August, 1864.

ASSISTANT SURGEONS.

Ormail L. Rider, Burton, Ohio, to May, 1863.

Henry B. Baker, Lansing, Mich., from August, 1864.

27th Michigan Infantry.

SURGEONS.

Cyrus M. Stockwell, Port Huron, Mich., to November, 1863.

Hamilton E. Smith, Detroit, Mich., from December, 1863.

ASSISTANT SURGEONS.

J. E. Davis, Macomb, Mich., to January, 1864.

James W. Niblack, Hillsdale, from January, 1864.

Benjamin E. Yarnold, from September, 1864.

H. H. Powers, to September, 1864.

Conclusion.

It will be evident to the readers that it has not been our great object to make generals' stars or colonels' eagles to shine more brightly and dazzlingly than they already do, but to show to them the sacrifices made by the men in the ranks who loaded and fired the guns, made or repulsed the deadly charge, and carried the nation's ensign through four years of fratricidal war with a valor unsurpassed, with a determination fixed and abiding, cost what it might— life, limb or rebel prison—the union of these States should be preserved. No greater proof is needed or can be given than that we already have—that the rank and file of the Union armies were patriots pure and simple, with unconquerable purpose that our Constitution and laws must be respected and obeyed, not one star should be stricken from the national escutcheon, that this great heritage of freedom should not be lost but handed down to the coming millions. The forty thousand dead and seventy thousand wounded who, under Grant, baptized the Old Dominion from the Rappahannock to the Appomattox with their blood, together with their comrades of other armies, forever consecrated this fair land to freedom and equal rights. When the few (comparatively) who still linger behind shall have pitched their tents on the other shore—when the last defender of the flag from 1861 to 1864 shall pass over and join the great majority, there will be heard millions of patriotic voices shouting:

> "How sleep the brave who sank to rest
> By all their country's wishes blest:
> By hands unseen their knell is rung,
> By forms unseen their dirge is sung.
> Honor comes in garb of grey
> To bless the turf that wraps their clay,
> And Freedom will awhile repair
> And dwell a willing hermit there."

APPENDIX.

AUGUSTUS C. FOX,
6th Michigan Cavalry.

APPENDIX.

I do not claim to have written a perfect history, but only what "I remember" in respect to the subjects mentioned concerning the great rebellion.

Many incidents of great interest to comrades have undoubtedly been omitted, but my prinpal object has been to give a correct history of the wounded brought to the field hospital of Michigan regiments in our division, the names of whom, with the nature of their injuries, have been carefully inserted, hoping it may prove of value to those whom the government has pledged its faith to help to *eke* out a more tolerable existence than otherwise could be obtained.

This volume will be found to be *strictly* authentic, and a *perfect copy* of the *reports* of our division hospital.

If we have one desire above another it is that we may be able to aid our suffering comrades in obtaining what is their due.

A Reunion.

On June 17, 1891, at a reunion (held at Hastings) of the 8th Michigan Infantry, it was resolved that we would meet on the 3d day of August, 1891, at Railroad Engineers' Hall, Detroit, Michigan, and that we would extend a reception to our old friends the 79th New York Highlanders.

The 79th sent us a telegram that they would meet us early on Monday afternoon, August 3, 1891.

The Cameron Club escorted us at 3 P. M. to the depot where we received our old friends.

General Morrison, though an invalid, was with us. Never in the history of men was a more gladsome meeting than we enjoyed as we clasped their dear old hands. Quarters had been secured for them by our old quartermaster, Major G. Chandler, at the Biddle House. Major Chandler is entitled to the lasting gratitude of his regiment for the splendid provision he made to entertain our old friends. The Cameron Club entertained us at their hall that evening where speeches were made by their president, responded to by General Morrison, and More and Laing of the 79th New York Highlanders, and Fox and Swinscoe and others of the 8th Michigan Infantry. It was one of those "feasts of reason and flow of soul" rarely enjoyed by men.

Mrs. Patterson rose and was greeted with cheers for the kindness and care she had manifested in regard to the graves of comrades. It is a very happy reflection to the 8th Michigan and 79th New York Highlanders that, although we left in Knoxville many very dear friends whom we were unable—for lack of transportation—to send home for burial, that this patriotic lady stands as sentinel, as it were, over their graves. The 8th Michigan left their drummer boy, CHARLIE, there. The 79th left many precious ones at Knoxville, and it is extremely gratifying to the comrades to feel assured that this lady does not forget them, and, as from year to year memorial day comes around, the fairest lillies of the valley bedeck our soldiers' graves.

It was resolved that the 79th New York Highlanders and the 8th Michigan Infantry shall hereafter be known as the First Brigade, First Division, Ninth Army Corps, and that General David Morrison be commander of the same. Adjutant E. H. Sawyer was duly elected, and hereafter the 8th Michigan Infantry and 79th New York Highlanders will be known as such.

Probably in the history of these men the meeting held at that hall was as interesting as any they had ever experienced.

These two old regiments "reunioning," after thirty years separation, who, during the war, were boys together, were now grey headed old men, and, as we witnessed them clasping each other's hands and observed the tears running down their cheeks, we knew their brave, patriotic hearts were being stirred to their lowest depths.

> Brave warriors, you have trod
> One hundred tented fields;
> Your battles all are fought,
>   Your victories all are won;
> Now, on your laurels rest
>   For all your work is done.

It was further resolved that we extend to Major General O. B. Wilcox at Washington, D. C., an invitation for October, 1892.

There is no doubt that occasions like the foregoing will be fraught with many interesting incidents relating to our old division.

The memory of General O. B. Wilcox will live ever green in the memory of the men who composed the first division of the Ninth Army Corps.

Comrade Hutchinson of the 79th New York Highlanders, being unable to visit us on that occasion, through sickness, sent a poem which we take pleasure in giving to the public.

The poem runs as follows:

> I can't find language to describe
>   The feelings of delight
> Which thrill our bosoms as we gaze
>   On old-time friends tonight;
> On dear old friends we thought to see
>   No more till Gabriel's horn
> Had blown the last assembly call
>   On Resurrection's morn;
> But our old comrades of the Eighth
>   Will no assurance need ·
> That to the Highlanders this hour
>   Is one of joy indeed;
> Without a word of mine they can,
>   By their own feelings, tell
> What glad emotions stir our hearts
>   At meeting, strong and well,
> So many of the men who stood,
>   Nigh thirty years ago,
> Beside us in our country's fight
>   Against the traitor foe.
>
> Of course not you nor we, in looks,
>   Are now as once we were,
> For Time, that grim Destroyer, does
>   Not youth nor beauty spare;

Our once thick locks of brown or black
    He's turned to white or gray,
And on some heads left not a hair
    To keep the flies away!
He's planted wrinkles 'round our eyes,
    And on our brows and necks,
And dimmed our vision, till we look
    Like owls behind our specs!
To some he's given stiffened joints,
    To others gave the gout,
And some endowed with double chins
    And "corporations" stout.
In fact, the Tyrant's done his best,
    Through all the bygone years,
To cripple those whom Death had spared
    From guns and swords and spears;
But little knew he of the stuff
    Of which our Vets were made—
The scabbard he might stain and dint,
    But couldn't dull the blade!

The fiery spirit that impelled
    Us to the deadly fray,
And through the toil of march and camp
    Bore us unflinchingly,
Is still unquenched, and burns as bright
    As in the olden days,
For "age is nothing—blood will tell,"
    As the old adage says.
And just to prove that what I say
    Is true, take Comrade Moore,

Our estimable President,
  And, tho' his hair is hoar,
And tho' Brazilian pebbles lend
  Assistance to his sight,
No one will dare assert that he
  Is not as spry and bright—
As full of fun and full of fire
  As three decades ago
When he the Beaufort Privateer,
  The "Wabash," took in tow!
Or when, with steady tread, he crept
  From out the sleeping camp
In search of a distillery
  For "drugs" to cure a cramp!
Or raided a reb farmer's grounds
  In chase of fowl or hog,
Regardless of the hayseed's gun
  Or of his savage dog.
Oh, no, he's just as frisky now
  As ever he was then,
And will be while he draws a breath—
And all the Cameron men
Are much the same as he,—for instance,
  Comrades Stewart and Baird
In soul and body feel as young
  As if they ne'er had shared
The hardships of a dreadful war;
  In fact so frolicsome
Are they that it was dangerous
  To let them go from home
Without their guardian angels

To protect them on the way
From all allurements that might lead
Their innocence astray(!).
The world has altered very much
Since Adam got a wife;
For, through her, he lost happiness
And endless earthly life;
But ever since, to make amends,
Her daughters, day and night,
Watch o'er their husbands lest they should
Go wrong when out of sight.
And any one who would object
To those dear angels' ward
Should be from every happiness
Eternally debarred.

Another of our veterans—
Glendenning is his name—
Sometimes called Ecclesfechan,
For there was whence he came—
Is also chock up full of fun,
Despite his cares and years,
Although, when one looks in his face
A deacon's "phiz" appears.
But by the binding you can't tell
What's inside of the book,
And often there's *diablerie*
Behind a saintly look!
And there's our comrade, Dr. Locke,
A man well on in years,
But young in spirit, tho' his work
Lies 'midst pain, groans and tears;

Grave and gentle is his face,
  But when he is unbent
Among his friends, he dosen't care
  A continental cent
For anything but jollity;
  Yet one would surely think
That he was not a jovial soul
  Because he doesn't drink !

There are some comrades, whom I'd like
  To name, who mock at Time;
And look as young and strong today
  As they did in their prime.
(As Armour, Dingwall, Crawford, Spence,
  Ewald, Grant, McLean,
Men stout enough and tough enough
  To go to war again.)
But if I spin my yarn too long
  About the Highlanders,
You'll think us egotistical,
  And likely close your ears.
My object in digressing from
  The subject matter was
To show how Time may age our frames,
  But can't our souls harass.

But now I'll hie me back to where
  I wandered from the way,
And tell our friends of Michigan
  How, from that distant day,
Now seven and twenty years ago,
  When we bade them farewell,

We've longed to see them once again
   Ere time had tolled our knell.
Yes, for reunion we have longed
   Through all the years since then,
Yet scarcely dared to hope that we
   Would our desire obtain.
But Heaven was gracious, and now, face to face,
   We meet those friends of thirty years ago—
For which our hearts are grateful.
   What a space
Of time's been passed
   Since battling with the foe.
We learned each others worth!
   Tho' to and fro,
East, west, north, south
   We trod with bleeding feet
Stern duty's thorny paths,
   We ne'er let go
The friendship then acquired;
   And, now, we meet
To-night, that friendship still
   Unbroken and complete.

Dear friends! Dear comrades! Eighth of Michigan!
What can I add to that already said,
But that our hearts with gladness overran
When first we knew of the arrangements made
To join our old companions on parade,
And at their hands receive a warm well-come
That would all other welcomes cast in shade,
And make the City of Detroit hum
With mingled yells and "Tigers" *ad infinitum!*

To meet with friends long parted's happiness,
But oh! the pleasure! to behold again
In life those friends who felt Death's cold embrace
At home, in camp, or on the battle plain.
Oh how we'd pierce the air with the refrain
Of "Comrades," did they bless our eyes tonight!
Alas! the thought's ridiculous and vain;
They would not leave their bowers of delight,
Even if they could, for earthly scenes, however bright.

If gallant Fenton and heroic Graves
Could bid adieu to fields Elysian,
And in old Charon's boat the Stygian waves
Recross, once more this earthly scene to scan,
And with them bring the shade of ev'ry man
Who fought with them and joined their ghostly train,—
What joy were ours, however brief the span
They'd be with us; and while they did remain
We'd treat them so they'd scarcely wish for Heav'n again.

Could valiant Stevens and the Highlanders
Who tread with him the paths all heroes tread
Return, for one brief night, to earthly cares,
Would we their ghostly presence shun in dread?
Ah, no! were they but here, though from the dead,
We'd give them hearty welcome, and rejoice
That, though their souls from earth had long since fled,
They yet such int'rest took in the "Old Boys"
That, for a while, they Heav'n forsook with all its joys!

Alas! those vanished ones will not return;
But we will go to them assuredly;

And, while we live we will their absence mourn,
And in our hearts enshrine their memory.
And now we'll leave them to His clemency
Who doeth all things well, and turn our thoughts
To living friends, and things sublunary,
To mirth and frolic, of which there are lots
When jolly Michiganders hob-nob with the Scots!

And now, dear friends, my pleasing task is done;
I've tried, howe'er imperfectly, to tell
With what regard for each and ev'ry one
Of the renowned "Old Eighth" our bosoms swell;
How much rejoiced to see, alive and well,
Old comrades, whom we thought no more to meet
Till Gabriel's trump had exorcised Death's spell,
And brought together, at the Mercy Seat,
Earth's parted ones, a union without end, complete.

WILLIAM HUTCHINSON.

MAJOR R. H. HENDERSHOT,
Drummer Boy of the Rappahannock, and his son.

THE DRUMMER BOY OF THE RAPPAHANNOCK.

The question whether Robert H. Hendershot is entitled to the cognomen of "Drummer Boy of the Rappahannock," which has been under discussion for some considerable time, has recently been presented to me, and, feeling sure the old soldiers would like to know the actual facts in the case, I present the naked truth, desiring justice should be done.

Many resolutions by large (civil as well as military) gatherings have been passed in respect to this matter, some supporting and others refuting his claim. I have, therefore, investigated the matter, and am enabled to give my readers his *true history* pertaining to that episode of his life.

In 1861 young Hendershot was a boy of about 11 years of age, living at Jackson, Mich.

At the commencement of the war, in company with Captain C. V. Deland and Kirk Purdy, he came to the 9th Michigan Infantry then lying at Fort Wayne. At that early period it appears that he was quite a good drummer, and Captain O. B. Rounds of Company B took charge of him.

When the regiment left Detroit for the front, Hendershot accompanied it, and remained with it as drummer boy until it was captured at Murfreesborough, July 13, 1862.

He seems to have been conspicuous wherever he went. In the battle at Murfreesborough, after beating the "long roll," he shouldered his gun and loaded and fired at the enemy with the coolness of a veteran.

After their surrender the 9th Michigan were marched to McMinnville and paroled; when they were sent to Camp Chase, Ohio, where Hendershot was discharged from the regiment. He then went to Detroit and re-enlisted under an assumed name (that of R. H. Henderson) in the 8th Michigan Infantry before he was exchanged, and remained several months at the recruiting station at Detroit in the capacity of drummer.

It appears from his history, which we have been able to obtain, he was a very restless boy, not easily to be controlled by any one, and, finding that the chaplain of the 8th Michigan Infantry was about to rejoin his regiment, then lying before Petersburg, Va., he besought him to take him along, which he did. On his arrival at the front he was assigned to Company B as drummer boy but never performed any duty in that capacity.

At this period his restless and uneasy disposition was manifested in a marked degree. A few days after his arrival the pontoons were laid across the river preparatory to the proposed attack on Lee's forces, who lay on Maire's Hill, just south of the city, and with the audacity peculiar to himself he went to the point where they were laying the pontoons, and as they were moving across the river the impulse seized him he must go too. Making a jump for one as it started he was unfortunate enough to miss it and drop into the water, but with his usual luck managed to seize the side of the boat and hang on until the other shore was reached. He soon made his way to the city, foraged a few trinkets and returned to his company.

After a short rest, his curiosity not being satisfied, he recrossed the river and, providing himself with a gun, went marching around to see what he could find. Entering a house, and going through to the back door, he discovered a rebel soldier in the yard, when, drawing a bead on him, he ordered him to surrender, which he did. This act of the boy of course delighted the soldiers, and a detail was quickly given to take him with his prisoner to the head quarters of General Burnside.

This daring act, although reckless in the extreme, deeply interested the General, and those about his headquarters, in the boy, who was cautioned not to cross the river again, which counsel he did not take, but returning to the south side received an ugly wound, upon which he was taken back again to General Burnside, where, his wound being dressed, as soon as was advisable he was sent to Washington, and from there to Providence, Rhode Island, the home of General Burnside.

His exploits at Fredericksburg, as would naturally be supposed, attracted the attention of newspaper correspondents, to whom he is, undoubtedly. indebted for the reputation he enjoys today.

At this time the attention of Horace Greely was called to him who generously presented to the young fellow a splendid silver drum (in commemoration of his daring act on the Rappahannock), at Cooper Institute, New York, from the hands of Major General Scott.

We conclude our remarks upon this matter by stating that the above facts are substantiated, not only by his discharge and other papers, but by statements made by Chaplain Taylor, General Burnside and a number of other prominent officers who were cognizant of the facts above stated, the evidences of which are in my possession.

That there were other drummer boys on active duty with their regiments at that time admits of no question.

"Charlie" Gardner, known personally to R. H. Hendershot, was there, as gallant a little fellow as ever beat a drum (and many others who deserve all the praise that a grateful country can bestow), who died as the accredited drummer boy of the 8th Michigan Infantry, pierced by a bullet while nobly and bravely carrying water to men in the trenches in front of Fort Sanders, Tenn.

The records in the Adjutant General's office at Lansing show that Robert H. Hendershot enlisted August 19, 1862, age 13, at Detroit, Mich., as drummer, Company B, 8th Michigan Infantry; joined regiment November 28, 1862, at Fredericksburg, Va.; discharged December 27, 1862, at Falmouth, Va., for disability, showing that he was in the service one month less one day.

John T. Spillane.

It is sharply maintained by many, who claim they were in a position to know, that Comrade John T. Spillane of Detroit, who enlisted as drummer of Company K, 7th Michigan Infantry, June 19, 1861, and enlisted a veteran December 18, 1863; wounded July 27, 1864, near Petersburg, Va., and again same day at Fort Haskell; mustered out July 5, 1865, at Jefferson Barracks, Ind., is the genuine Drummer Boy of the Rappahannock.

These witnesses are sustained by strong evidence that he beat his drum in the van of his regiment, which was the first to cross the pontoon bridge, December 12, 1862, and continued to do so until one of the heads of his drum was knocked in by a piece of shell

It is not claimed by Mr. Hendershot or his friends that he even had a drum while with the 8th Michigan Infantry.

We have thus given the facts of the matter in contention, hoping the question will be settled amicably and that the most deserving will wear the honor of Drummer Boy of the Rappahannock.

INDEX.

	PAGE.
A heavy battle raging	104
A. Johnson, Tailor	23
A legacy	206
A limb of the law	44
A ludicious scene	45
A peg in the wheel	190
Assassination of Lincoln	194
At Annapolis	48
Attached to the first brigade	18
A weary journey	64
Battle of Blue Springs	22
Battle of Five Forks	186
Battle of Sailor's Creek	190-191
Battle of Weldon R. R.	144-148
Beaufort	17
Bethesda church	89
Boys, let us have rest	103
Brickyard Point	17
Bulldog grip	163
Captain Roemer	30
Captain R. M. Doyle	50
Captain John C. Buchanan	53
Captain Donahue and Lieutenant Hovey wounded	67
Captain Hutchinson	63
Charge at Cold Harbor	90
Colonel Ely	51
Colonel Graves in the mill pond	53-54
Commissioned officers mustered out	245-252
Complaints made to Gen. Burnside	38
Comrades we left behind	47
Crossing the James	103
Cumberland Gap	38
Danford Parker	46
Death of Major Belcher	149
Delos Warner	40
Doctor Bonine	64
Doctor Vickery	143

	PAGE.
"Drive Jones out of those woods"	23
Duties performed	22
East Tennessee	28
Eighth Michigan Infantry, when and where formed	13
Efforts to break Lee's line at Poplar Grove church	149
Emancipation Proclamation	152
Explosion of the mine	143
Extreme restlessness	201
Field and staff	14
Field Hospital	178
First campaign in Virginia	20
Gathering up the wounded	193
General Cox's report	19
Generals Mead and Sheridan	70
General Wilcox to the aid of Warren	144
Graves at Campbell Station	28
Greenville, Tenn.	23
Guarding government property	198
Harris House	69
Heavy rains and bad roads	192
Hilton Head	10
Held his fort	33
Important records	70
In camp at Annapolis, Md.	49
In camp at Louden	26
In camp at Milldale	20
In front of Petersburg	104
In Washington	198
Lieutenant Belcher	19
Lieutenant Benjamin	31
Lieutenant Porter	17
Lincoln and Seward on the River Queen	165
Longstreet's corps and the Ninth corps	34
Losses at Spottsylvania	68
Major W. E. Lewis	24-25
Making shoes of rawhide	37
Martin Decker	43
Minute guns	196
Mobile and Alabama railroad	22
Morristown, East Tenn.	22
Move to Kentucky	20

INDEX. 277

	PAGE.
Must not be thwarted	179
My country, 'tis of thee	203
Names of company officers	14-15
Newport News	18
No rations	24
Number of enlisted men	16
On board steamer "Honduras"	18
Off for Michigan	204
Oppressive duties	162
Order to keep close up	180
Paid no attention to their complaints at the Adams' House	182
"Papa" Ely	177
Passing brick	26
Phil. a raging lion	183
Presented with a flag	17
Presidential election	151
Private soldiers, not fools	189
Re-enlisted	35
Reported for duty	12
Resolutions drafted and read to the 79th N. Y.	36
Retreat to Knoxville and Louden	25
Reviewed by General Grant	48
Reviewed by the President	52
Root hog or die	167
Roster Eighth Michigan Infantry	230-244
Sacrifices made	23
Seventy-ninth New York and 8th Michigan Infantry	27
Sheridan	172
Sherman at Savannah	155
Sick in field hospital	208-220
Slavery abolished	153
Slippery Mountains	41
Spottsylvania	67
Stevens, Campbell and Hunter	104
Struck the last hospital tent	195
Swinging by the left	178
"Tell the sutler to get out"	39
Tenth Michigan Cavalry	42
The decree executed	188
The grip tightening	181
The Morning Dawn	168
The world had laughed	154

	PAGE.
Twenty-fourth N. Y. cavalry	65
Twenty thousand miles	22
Tying up a captain	200
Under Major Ralph Ely	19
Warren did not come	185
Warren relieved	187
Weighed down with anxiety	33
When and where engaged with the enemy	16
When the regiment left Annapolis	16
When the regiment left Detroit	16
Wilcox and Hartranft, the Pride of the Corps	169
Wilmington Island	18
Wounded at Cold Harbor	92-101
Wounded at Fall of Petersburg	158-161
Wounded at North Anna	86-88
Wounded at Petersburg	105-142
Wounded at Poplar Grove church	150
Wounded at Spottsylvania	72-81
Wounded at Weldon R. R.	144
Wounded of the battle of the Wilderness	56-62
Wounded on picket	156-157
Wounded sent to City Point	187
Wounded, 1st Michigan S. S.	85

ILLUSTRATIONS.

Augustus C. Fox.
E. J. Bonine, M. D., Surgeon 2d Michigan Infantry.
Honorable W. M. Fenton, Colonel 8th Michigan 1862.
Hulburt B. Shank, Surgeon 8th Michigan to 1862.
Jefferson Kent.
Major Horatio Belcher, killed August 19, 1864.
Ralph Ely, Colonel 8th Michigan Infantry 1865.
Wells B. Fox, M. D., Surgeon 8th Michigan Infantry.
Wm. Ely Lewis, Major to 1864.

APPENDIX.

Drummer Boy of the Rappahannock	269
Poem by Hutchinson	261

www.ingramcontent.com/pod-product-compliance
Lightning Source LLC
Chambersburg PA
CBHW030020240426
43672CB00007B/1026